Controversial Issues in Social Welfare Policy

Government
and the Pursuit
of Happiness

Carl P. Chelf

Controversial Issues in Public Policy
Volume 3

SAGE Publications
International Educational and Professional Publisher
Newbury Park   London   New Delhi

For information address:

SAGE Publications, Inc.
2455 Teller Road
Newbury Park, California 91320

SAGE Publications Ltd.
6 Bonhill Street
London EC2A 4PU
United Kingdom

SAGE Publications India Pvt. Ltd.
M-32 Market
Greater Kailash I
New Delhi 110 048 India

Printed in the United States of America

Library of Congress Cataloging-in-Publication Data

Chelf, Carl P.
    Controversial issues in social welfare policy: Government and
the pursuit of happiness / Carl P. Chelf.
        p.   cm.—(Controversial issues in public policy; v. 3)
    Includes bibliographical references and index.
    ISBN 0-8039-4042-4.—ISBN 0-8039-4043-2 (pbk.)
    1. Public welfare—United States.   2. United States—Social
policy—1980-   I. Title.   II. Series.
    HV95.C43   1992   92-29501
361.6'1'0973—dc20   CIP

93 94 95 10 9 8 7 6 5 4 3 2

Sage Production Editor: Judith L. Hunter

1995

Controversial Issues in Social Welfare Policy

CONTROVERSIAL ISSUES IN PUBLIC POLICY

Series Editors
Dennis Palumbo and Rita Mae Kelly
Arizona State University

Volume 1   **CONTROVERSIAL ISSUES IN ENVIRONMENTAL POLICY**
Science vs. Economics vs. Politics
KENT E. PORTNEY

Volume 2   **CONTROVERSIAL ISSUES IN ENERGY POLICY**
ALFRED A. MARCUS

Volume 3   **CONTROVERSIAL ISSUES IN SOCIAL WELFARE POLICY**
Government and the Pursuit of Happiness
CARL P. CHELF

Volume 4   **CONTROVERSIAL ISSUES IN EDUCATIONAL POLICY**
LOUANN A. BIERLEIN

Volume 5   **CONTROVERSIAL ISSUES IN HEALTH CARE POLICY**
JENNIE J. KRONENFELD

Volume 6   **CONTROVERSIAL ISSUES IN ECONOMIC REGULATORY POLICY**
MARCIA LYNN WHICKER

Contents

Series Editors' Introduction
Rita Mae Kelly and Dennis Palumbo   vii

1 The Federal Government and Social Welfare Policy   1
   Changes in Attitudes and Role   2
   Major Issues in Social Welfare Policy   4
   The Conservative Position   6
   The Liberal Position   9
   The Current Setting   13
   Social Welfare in the Future   17
   Conclusion   17

2 Reducing Poverty's Sting   21
   The War on Poverty   27
   Efforts at Solution   30
   Conclusion   37

3 Hunger in America   41
   Major Issues   46
   Efforts at Solution   50
   Conclusion   52

4   Homeless in America   57

    Public Housing   64
    Major Issues   65
    Addressing the Housing Problem   67
    Conclusion   73

5   Jobs: Protection, Promotion, Training, Assistance   76

    Major Issues   77
    Efforts at Solution   79
    Conclusion   102

6   Helping Children and Families   108

    Background   108
    Major Issues   116
    Efforts at Solution   118
    Conclusion   127

7   The Continuing Search for Social Policies That Work   133

    Future Directions   138

  References   146

  Index   153

  About the Author   160

Series Editors' Introduction

Public policy controversies escalated during the 1980s and early 1990s. This was partly due to bitter partisan debate between Republicans and Democrats, a "divided" government in which the Republicans controlled the presidency and the Democrats controlled the Congress, and the rise of "negative" campaigning in the 1988 presidential election. In addition, highly controversial issues such as abortion, crime, environmental pollution, affirmative action, and choice in education became prominent on the public policy agenda in the 1980s.

Policy issues in this atmosphere tend to be framed in dichotomous, either-or terms. Abortion is depicted as murder on the one hand and a woman's self-interested choice on the other. One is either tough on crime or too much in favor of defendants' rights. Affirmative action is a matter of quotas or a special interest issue. School choice is the means for correcting the educational "mess," or the destruction of public education. In such a situation there seems to be no middle or common ground in which cooler heads can unite.

The shrillness of these policy disputes reduces the emphasis on finding rational, balanced solutions. Political ideology and a zero-sum approach to politics and policy became the order of the day.

Certainly, there has been no "end to ideology" since the beginning of the 1980s, as some believed was occurring in the 1970s. Instead "Reaganomics" contributed to a widening gap between the rich and the poor and this seemed to exacerbate partisan debate and further stymie governmental action. In 1992, controversies over health care—lack of coverage for millions and skyrocketing costs—illustrate the wide gap in the way Republicans and Democrats approach public policy controversies. The Reagan "revolution" was based on a definite and clear ideological preference for a certain approach to public policy in general: eliminate government regulation, reduce taxes, provide tax incentives for business, cut welfare, and privatize the delivery of governmental services. Democrats, of course, did not agree.

This series, Controversial Issues in Public Policy, is meant to shed more light and less ideological heat on major policy issues in the substantive policy areas. In this volume, Carl P. Chelf examines social welfare policy in the United States, focusing on issues of poverty, homelessness, hunger, unemployment, underemployment, disability, the elderly, and aid to needy children and families. The controversies over whether social welfare programs do more harm than good are illuminated by his review of available data and assessments of national progress. Chelf notes that the proportion of poor in the U.S. population declined from 22.4% in 1959 to 12.8% in 1989. Nonetheless, debate still rages between those who argue for more individualism, self-reliance, and strengthening of the work ethic and those who argue for a more egalitarian society with justice, fairness, and basic well-being for all its members. Controversy over the proper role of government in promoting public welfare permeates the debates. The Reagan-Bush era featured renewed emphases on voluteerism, private charity, and a "trickle-down" theory of how the poor can be helped. Federal government involvement was said to promote fraud, waste, and abuse. Social spending bred, it was argued, dependency, great national debt, and weakened families. Yet the ideological conservatism was belied by an operational liberalism as both federal and local spending increased during the Reagan-Bush era. At least half of all U.S. households benefit from welfare programs, whether they are social insurance programs protecting against ill health, old age, and a weak economy, or assistance programs aiding the needy. This tension between our rhetoric and reality is documented by Chelf, and the trends in U.S. social welfare policy are illuminated. Of broad interest is the emphasis placed throughout the book on the continued need to reassess and reformulate public policy to meet changing demographic and economic reality.

RITA MAE KELLY
DENNIS PALUMBO

1

The Federal Government and
Social Welfare Policy

A mericans have been persistently ambivalent about the federal government's role in social welfare policy. Although subscribing strongly
to the ideas of social justice and the government's role in promoting
that objective, they believe equally as strongly in the concepts of
individualism and capitalistic free enterprise, which often may conflict
with the government's social role.

Despite the Declaration of Independence's proclamation, "That to secure these rights, Governments are instituted among Men," and Madison's
statement in *Federalist* No. 51 that "Justice is the end of government,"
Americans were much slower than Europeans to accept a broader
"social welfare" role for government. The term "welfare state" was used
in Europe in the late 1800s and early 1900s, but Americans harbored a
strong aversion to the term. Although accepting as a legitimate function
of the national government the promotion of the welfare of the community as a whole and realizing also that the welfare of individual citizens
was related to that of society as a whole, for many "social role" still
meant "the dole," "welfarism," and "paternalism." Those activities that
directly advanced the economic and social well-being of individuals
and families were still viewed as primarily the responsibilities of
private charities and philanthropic organizations or state and local

1

governments. In 1838 James Fenimore Cooper observed, "The American nation is a great nation, in some particulars, the greatest the world ever saw, . . . but . . . it is lamentably in arrears to its own avowed principles" (Chisman & Pifer, 1987, p. 119).

Changes in Attitudes and Role

Article I, Section 8, of the U.S. Constitution grants to Congress the authority to levy taxes for promoting "the general welfare," but federal involvement in welfare policy was quite limited until the start of the 20th century. Throughout our early history most social welfare needs were addressed largely by families, voluntary organizations, and local governments. As recently as 1928, the eve of the Great Depression, only about 12% of the relief provided in 15 of the country's largest cities came from public funds. It was still widely believed that the "really needy" could be taken care of sufficiently through private philanthropy.

With the onset of the Great Depression in 1929, this traditional approach was simply not equal to the task and crumbled under the weight of mounting needs. Traditional concepts of poverty and need were put to the test as some degree of economic hardship and deprivation struck just about everyone at all levels of society. Bank and business failures were widespread, unemployment hit 20%, and those fortunate enough to have jobs often earned barely enough to survive. Even middle-class Americans were forced into the soup and bread lines. Suddenly it was driven home quite forcefully that poverty could be a result of flaws in the economic system just as well as of those of individual character.

Out of this experience emerged a greatly expanded federal social role as the government displayed a real concern for the welfare of its citizens suffering from the ravages of the Great Depression. This was manifested in conscious and deliberate policies creating new forms of social support designed to help reduce the economic uncertainties of citizens in several areas. That a national response was necessary was pretty well conceded, the primary question regarding federal involvement becoming how much and in whose behalf.

The Great Depression pointed up some serious flaws in the country's economic and social structures, prompting President Franklin Roosevelt to offer the observation, "Government in the past has helped lay the foundation of business and industry. We must face the fact that in this century we have a rich man's security and a poor man's security and the government owes equal obligation to both" (Chisman & Pifer, 1987, p. 39).

Roosevelt appointed the Committee on Economic Security, headed by his secretary of Labor, Frances Perkins. A 50-page report by this committee became the charter for the emerging federal social welfare role. The cornerstone for the federal welfare state was laid with the adoption of the Social Security Act of 1935, which had two basic components: a system of social insurance based on employee/employer contributions and a noncontributory program of social assistance. Once the basic underpinnings were in place, a broad range of unmet human and social needs gradually were placed on the national policy agenda.

The Great Depression and World War II bolstered confidence in the government's problem-solving abilities, and following the war social welfare policy came to be viewed as the government's attempt to ensure the economic and social well-being of its citizens. This viewpoint, coupled with an unprecedented period of prosperity, advances in social science research, and the emergence of organized groups to push the issues, produced numerous additions to the federal social role—the GI Bill, public housing, employee benefits, pensions, health insurance, school lunches, food stamps, and others. The culmination of this move-ment was President Lyndon Johnson's massive War on Poverty in the 1960s, with its host of social welfare efforts.

By the 1970s, however, social welfare efforts began to falter as the result of a number of factors. Just as the Great Depression and World War II had fostered confidence in governmental institutions and their problem-solving efforts, the Vietnam War and the Watergate scandal badly eroded confidence. Also the post-World War II economic growth had begun to slow by the 1970s, producing little growth in real income. Because most of the expanded efforts of the previous decades had been funded from revenues produced through economic growth rather than new taxes (see Aaron, 1990; Chisman & Pifer, 1987), people now became much more reluctant to pay the bills of a socially active national government. In addition, program shortcomings and mismanagement led to growing misgivings on the part of many about such social efforts. In one study, the Ford Foundation noted that some programs were poorly conceived and promised more than could realistically be deliv-ered. Others, it reported, were poorly implemented, and some aimed at broadening opportunity actually fostered dependency (Ford Founda-tion, 1989b).

The decades of the 1970s and 1980s witnessed widespread criticism of the federal social welfare role, and a growing number of critics charged that social welfare programs were a failure. The government, they maintained, was not the answer to the nation's social problems, but was itself the major problem. The resurgent New Right viewed social expenditures as harmful to individual initiative and free competition and therefore counter to the central concepts of a free enterprise capitalistic system. They advocated a return to the free market, the family, and private charity as the major providers of welfare services.

The mounting criticism against social welfare programs and the economic declines in the 1980s paved the way for Ronald Reagan's efforts to reduce the federal role in these areas. A 1980 presidential commission report recommended complete federalization of the welfare system, for example, returning more responsibility to the individual states. Consequently, efforts were made—not totally successfully—to shift social service programs to the states through block grants. Reagan also tried to reduce some programs by tightening eligibility requirements, as with disability benefits in 1981. Also in 1981, food stamp recipients were required to seek work or be dropped. In 1982 Reagan proposed that social security benefits be reduced, but he quickly encountered strong opposition. Well over half of government-funded social services are delivered by private, nonprofit institutions; under Reagan these efforts also were substantially curtailed. Renee Berger, president of Teamworks, a firm working with nonprofit groups, noted, "In the past, the federal government took the traditional role of funding nonprofit efforts and experiments. Under Reagan, government walked away from that role" (Steinbach, 1988, p. 3192). Others also reported that many private groups dealing with housing, community development, social services, civil rights, the handicapped, employment, and job training barely scraped by in the 1980s.

Major Issues in Social Welfare Policy

Welfare policies are an issue on which rational and intelligent people can and do hold a wide range of often conflicting opinions. Disagreement over such policies is both philosophical and practical. Although the decades since the Great Depression have produced a substantial national welfare state, it rests on quite conflicting ideological underpinnings. It is an irrefutable reality, but ideologically it remains only marginally acceptable for many. Some of the most fundamental ideas held by Americans that come to bear on social welfare policies involve a dichotomy. Among the most widely embraced American ideas is that of individual freedom and equality of opportunity—the fundamental guarantee of life, liberty, and the pursuit of happiness. Also deeply imbedded in American belief is the idea of *progress*—that society can be improved and that individuals through hard work and perseverance can improve their own lot in society. This strong belief in individualism, coupled with equally strong beliefs in economic freedom and a free market capitalistic economy, influence heavily the debates over social welfare policies.

Capitalism, with its emphasis on hard work and individual initiative, suggests that poverty is the result of a person's unwillingness to work or to work hard enough. Many Americans tend to be suspicious of anyone who cannot provide for him/herself; they hold strong convictions that everyone willing to put forth the appropriate effort can and should be self-supporting through work. They remain convinced that opportunity is there for those willing to seize it and have yet to accept the idea that despite best efforts, some able-bodied adults in our society simply are unable to earn a decent living. Consequently, there remains widespread resistance to providing public support to able-bodied adults unless such benefits are "earned." In *Government for the People,* Chisman and Pifer (1987) observed that the idea of individualism has helped to legitimize programs that benefit most those who are best able to achieve security through their own efforts and stigmatizes those programs that are for persons least able to help themselves (p. 145).

Another perception strong among the more conservative elements in U.S. society is that the private sector is inherently more efficient, more productive, and somehow more responsive to public demands than government. This idea, coupled with the bias of many Americans against major social efforts by the national government, has also shaped the debate on social welfare policies. Many observers continue to view the federal role as being primarily to supplement the efforts of families, charities, and other levels of government. Those holding such views feel much of the federal role in this realm could and should be privatized. President Bush's "thousand points of light" concept reflects this belief (Bush, 1989). Early in his political career Senator Orrin Hatch (R., UT) observed, "In a wealthy society such as ours, we should take care of the sick, the infirm, the disabled and the handicapped. Private charity is the best way to do this, and government the worst" (*Review of the News,* 1978). In June 1989, addressing colleagues on behalf of the proposed Act for Better Child Care Services, of which he was a cosponsor, Senator Hatch said, "I think it is important that we face the responsibilities we have to help families who really cannot help themselves" (*Review of the News,* 1978). Although Senator Hatch has modified his position, many others remain convinced that social programs ought largely be left to private enterprise, charity, families, and voluntarism. They maintain that governmental efforts tend only to undermine private initiative and individual responsibility.

The Conservative Position

Many conservatives see social programs for the poor as actually doing more harm than good. They claim such programs are ineffective and a waste of taxpayers' dollars. Furthermore, if benefits are generous, they may become an incentive for people to quit working and take a free ride. This latter concern is a major reason why welfare benefits in the United States have been kept quite low. Many Americans tend to see two classes of poor: deserving and undeserving. Although willing to help the former, many people resent those who they feel are capable of supporting themselves.

Conservatives also contend that social programs redistribute income to people who either don't need it or don't deserve it, and many such as Charles Murray, George Gilder, and Irving Kristol, as well as groups like the Business Roundtable, the National Association of Manufacturers, and the U.S. Chamber of Commerce, along with conservative think tanks such as the Heritage Foundation, the Hoover Institute, and the National Bureau of Economic Research, maintain that social welfare programs are riddled with fraud, waste, and abuse. Those subscribing to these views charge that social programs generally have proven ineffective in achieving their goals, cost far too much, and are largely a waste of the taxpayers' dollars. Some opponents to such expenditures claim that federal spending for social purposes has grown so large that it is harmful to the overall economy and any further social spending would produce disastrous effects. In his 1988 book *On Borrowed Time: How the Growth in Entitlement Spending Threatens America's Future,* Peter Peterson, for example, decried federal entitlement programs as "part of our public compulsion to spend more than we earn, to consume more than we produce and to pass the hidden check on to those too innocent to understand what is at stake" (Kosterlitz, 1988b, p. 3160). Some conservative critics oppose social welfare programs because they insist such programs breed dependency and sap ambition. These programs create a class of dependent persons, the critics charge, and then sustain them in their dependency. Ralph Segalman and David Marsland, authors of *Cradle to Grave*(1989), argue that excessive state welfare fractures the family and creates generations of children incapable of life on their own. Such tendencies run counter to traditional American beliefs in the virtue of individual self-reliance and earning one's own subsistence.

These critics further contend that the poverty issue is exaggerated by the government and those pushing poverty relief programs. George Gilder contends that poverty is seen as both more extreme and more remediable than it really is (Gilder, 1990). Those pushing this view maintain that if in-kind benefits (food stamps, medicaid, rent subsidies) were counted as a part of income, the percentage of the population living below the poverty level would be reduced from over 13% to about 10%. These critics charge that many of those classified as poor really are not all that poor. They point out that in 1989 among those classified as poor by the Census Bureau, 38% owned their homes; over 60% owned a car and 14% two or more; over half had air conditioning in their homes, over 30% had microwave ovens; and 22,000 had heated swimming pools or hot tubs.

Charging that current policies are all wrong, George Gilder (1990) insists that the only way out of poverty for most people is "work, family and faith" (p. 661). The current poor refuse to work hard, he says, and one of the main reasons is that present programs pay them not to do so. If they are to escape their poverty, not only must the poor work, says Gilder; they must work harder than the classes above them. Current programs have also weakened the family and this is a major factor in the poverty of many. "The key to the intractable poverty of the hardcore American poor is the dominance of single and separated men in poor communities," Gilder charged:

> Once a family is headed by a woman, it is almost impossible for it to greatly raise its income even if the woman is highly educated and trained. . . . Her family responsibilities and distractions tend to prevent her from the kind of all-out commitment that is necessary for the full use of earning

power. Few women with children make earning money the top priority in
their lives. (p. 662)

Therefore, he wrote, "The first priority of any serious program against
poverty is to strengthen the male role in poor families" (p. 663).

Critics such as Gilder tend to discount the income gap between the
rich and poor and oppose programs that are strongly redistributive.
Efforts to take income from the rich and give it to the poor will simply
curtail the investments of the former and reduce the work incentives of
the latter, according to Gilder. This will cut productivity, reduce job
opportunities, and perpetuate the poverty of the poor. Instead, to improve the incomes of the poor, the government needs to increase
investment, which means increasing the wealth of the wealthy: Increasing income inequality will improve the economic lot of the poor as well
as the rich (p. 661).

These critics also see government social policies as contributing to
the problems of minorities. The idea that racism and discrimination
account for the lower incomes and high poverty rates among blacks is,
according to Gilder (1990), "At once false and invidious" (p. 661). Like
Gilder, Thomas Sowell does not see current policies as the solution, but
as sometimes complicating the problems. He feels the answer to poverty
among blacks can best be achieved by their gaining greater family
stability and embracing middle-class moral values (Sowell, 1990b).

Because a major portion of spending to reduce poverty has been
targeted at the elderly, they also have become a target of the critics of
social spending. The critics point out that although the elderly constitute less than 12% of the nation's population, they consume 28% of the
national budget and 51% of the social services expenditures. Since
1960, federal spending on programs benefiting the elderly has grown
from 6% of the budget to 28%, or a total outlay of over $300 billion
annually. The elderly currently receive approximately 75% of the benefits from entitlement programs.

A consequence of the government's increased spending on programs
benefiting the elderly has been a change in their public image. Earlier
they were generally seen as universally poor and relatively powerless
politically. Suddenly they are perceived as universally affluent and a
potent force politically. The *New York Times* frequently refers to social
security recipients as "the monied classes." *Forbes* magazine observed
of the elderly, "The reality is that they are living well" and "the trouble
is there are too many of them."

Others share the perception that the elderly more and more are benefiting from a system that rewards them disproportionately regardless of their financial status. In 1985 the President's Council of Economic Advisors announced that the elderly were "no longer a disadvantaged group" (Minkler, 1990, p. 98), providing more fuel for the critics' attacks. The critics charge that the elderly are one of the wealthiest segments of society and therefore should not be benefiting so heavily from federal programs. They point out that three out of four families whose members are over age 65 own their own homes, most with mortgages already paid off. Those in households whose members are 65 or older also own 40% of the nation's financial assets and can hardly be regarded as poor, contend the critics. Some charge that current policies are bankrupting the younger generation through excessive spending on programs to benefit the elderly, many of whom don't need the benefits. If the current trend continues, economist Milton Friedman predicts a "revolt of the young against the old." Several of those opposing increased social spending for the elderly have founded Americans for Generational Equity (AGE). This group is heavily supported by the insurance industry and several major defense contractors such as General Dynamics, TRW, Rockwell International, ITT and U.S. Steel. Interestingly, AGE charges that the nation's future "has been sold to the highest bidder among pressure groups and special interest." AGE's critics have labeled the group the "yuppie lobby" and "granny bashers."

The Liberal Position

Liberals defend an active social welfare role for the federal government and reject many of the conservative arguments, of course. Chisman and Pifer (1987) pointed out that Lincoln's famous statement on government "of and by" the people, is also "for the people." They maintain that the federal social role is "an idea and a tradition of government." The government, they maintain, has used that role "to provide a level of personal security that corporate America, voluntary associations, and most individuals acting on their own could never afford—against the hazards of old age, unemployment, disability and other forms of hardship" (p. 18). Those embracing the liberal viewpoint tend to see social welfare policies as the legitimate function of a government that cares about the welfare of its citizens. Neal R. Peirce

(1988) noted, "Privatization may be a great idea, but it's no substitute for a government that cares" (p. 138). Former U.S. Senator Tom Eagleton (D., MO) wrote (1982) in *The Atlantic* magazine, "A decent society tries to solve its pressing problems even when they directly afflict only a limited sector of the population" (p. 8).[1]

Liberal defenders of the social welfare role maintain that under the democratic concept of equality government has an obligation to look out for the welfare of *all* of its citizens. Although equality of opportunity may legitimately produce inequality of outcomes and results, the government is still obliged to seek equality in the institutions of society and to ensure the rights of all persons to equality of treatment by the government. The concept of equality also involves the idea of fairness, and although those who are employed may question why they should pay taxes to provide benefits for those who are not working, this begs the issue of society's obligation to those who are quite willing to work, but cannot find jobs or are forced to accept wages that fail to provide them a decent living. Proponents of social welfare maintain that the government must intervene to provide a degree of equity for these elements of the population (see Dobelstein, 1990).

Responding to the critics' claim that social programs are primarily the responsibility of the private sector, liberal defenders of the governments's role point out that it was the failure of private sector efforts that led to such government programs over the years. The free market economy, they contend, sometimes fails for everyone and more frequently for certain elements of our society. This makes it necessary for the government to intervene and ameliorate the effects of such failures in the capitalistic system. The defenders of government social programs also maintain that policymakers feel there are limits to how much responsibility the private sector can be asked to assume in solving such problems and they are reluctant to ask them to do more and more.

The proponents of federal social programs charge that the critics tend to couch spending for such efforts in terms of winners and losers: the rich supporting the poor, the working supporting the nonworking, and the young supporting the elderly. This, they maintain, is wrong, because over the long run everyone benefits from such programs because they improve society as a whole. Nor, they point out, do most economists see spending on these programs as a major threat to the national economy. After all, they explain, while social spending was rising from the 1960s to the 1980s, effective corporate tax rates and the marginal tax rate for high-income persons actually declined. Therefore, they maintain, spending on social programs was not the drain on the economy its critics often contend.

Liberal proponents of programs to aid the poor and their critics also tend to disagree as to the extent of the problem and the best methods for responding. Critics charge that the Census Bureau's numbers of poor people are inflated, but proponents maintain that the numbers of those living in or near poverty may be even higher. They also question the critics' claim that in-kind contributions should be calculated in determining the income of welfare recipients. Such contributions, they point out, may not actually increase available income at all, and in the case of medical assistance may not even cover all the medical expenses incurred.

Proponents and opponents also disagree as to the relationship of aid to the poor and work. Proponents point out that today poorer households are more likely than in the past to be headed by a working-age adult. Studies show that one half of those living in poverty have at least one member of the family working at least part-time, two thirds of these full-time. Defenders of the programs also point out the lack of any conclusive evidence that income maintenance programs discourage recipients from working. In fact, they maintain, most evidence from empirical research indicates that income maintenance is not a disincentive to work. The Coalition on Human Needs reported that in its interviews with 50 poor or near-poor, three fourths were or had at some time received benefits but most wanted to work and had worked at one time or another (Kosterlitz, 1989b, p. 90). The poor, their defenders point out, encounter numerous obstacles in their efforts to improve their lives through work. They are usually less educated than other workers and less skilled. The jobs that are available for them are often low-paying, dead-end, seasonal, part-time, or spot employment, in many cases providing few or no benefits beyond the low pay. In many cases taking the job available may not be economically feasible because of the costs for child care, transportation, and other factors. Putting the poor to work, point out those defending current efforts, requires a whole range of complex and costly support services such as education, job training, family counseling, child care, etc. For a vast majority of the poor, jobs are not a viable alternative because they are too young, too old, or too sick or disabled to work. Approximately 70% of those living below the poverty line are actually unable to work.

Poverty, contend the liberals, is a vicious circle that must be broken if those in its grip are to improve their lot. Poverty deprives both parents and children of the opportunity to succeed and improve their lives. "It's not [that the poor] can't set their own priorities," noted Congressman Augustus Hawkins (D., CA), chairman of the House Education and Labor Committee; "it's that their condition dictates what their priorities are" (Kosterlitz, 1989c, p. 1110). The Center for Social Policy Studies of the Ford Foundation (1989a) reported, "The poor tend to suffer more than their share of social ills: family breakups, teen pregnancies, inadequate housing, and ill health." Female-headed families, noted the foundation report, are even more likely than other poor families to be deluged in such problems. The poor, explain their defenders, are usually much less equipped to cope and bounce back when adversity strikes. As Michael Harrington observed, "Their entire environment, their life, their values, do not prepare them to take advantage of the new opportunity" (Harrington, 1990, p. 651). Consequently, they require more than just a job and welfare benefits; they need "personal support" as well.

Responding to the criticisms directed toward programs for the elderly, liberals point out that without social security the poverty rate among older Americans would increase nearly fourfold, forcing them to depend on their children, relatives, private charities, or welfare for support. Social security, they maintain, has lifted over 9 million elderly out of poverty. Defenders of programs for the elderly charge the critics with ignoring the tremendous income variations within the elderly cohort. Many of the analysts most critical of these programs, they claim, deal with average income figures for those over 65 that gloss over large pockets of poverty among certain categories of elderly.

To the charge that the elderly are mortgaging the future of the younger generation and that in a reversal of the traditional pattern retirees now may earn more than the workers supporting the programs, liberals respond that this should instead be an argument for raising the incomes of those at the lower end of the scale. Defenders of income maintenance programs chide the critics for playing the younger generation against the older. Social policy is not a zero-sum game, they maintain, and cutting assistance to one group does not automatically result in more benefits for another. Many young people also benefit from social security, they add, and all generations have a stake in social welfare programs. Actually, argue the liberals, poor people benefit less from the social spending programs than do members of the middle class. Poor people benefit less from the contributory programs such as social security, unemployment insurance, and Medicare and have to rely more on the noncontributory programs such as Supplemental Security Income (SSI), Aid to Families With Dependent Children (AFDC), and medicaid, where benefits are kept low. Furthermore, the advocates for poverty relief contend, the poor in our society should be viewed as an undeveloped resource. By helping them break the bonds of their poverty, the whole society can benefit from reduced crime, increased spending and productivity, economic growth, and reduced expenditures on welfare.

The Current Setting

Twenty-six years of unprecedented economic growth and prosperity following World War II allowed the federal government to expand its social role, providing education and housing assistance for the returning GIs and expanding the social security base by adding disability insurance, Medicare, and Medicaid. Efforts were launched on many other fronts as well. By the 1970s and 1980s, however, economic growth had slowed; Vietnam, Watergate, and the energy crisis had eroded confidence in government; and the civil rights, women's rights, and affirmative action efforts had created a backlash. Critics of the government's social efforts, such as George Gilder (1981), Charles Murray (1984), and Thomas Sowell (1981), found a widely receptive audience.

Currently our social welfare system is undergoing close scrutiny as new developments threaten to overwhelm a system that was created and developed in an environment when social and economic conditions were entirely different. Policymakers are carefully reviewing the federal social role, looking for measures that will fit the changed environment and at the same time respond to widespread public discontent.

As we enter the 1990s we face a time of unprecedented changes, many of which pose serious challenges for social welfare policies. Our population is growing older and living longer, and older people require more social services. In 1986, 26% of Americans were 55 or older; 12.5% were at least 65; and 41% of the elderly population were 75 or older. The average age of our population will continue to climb in the 1990s, and by the turn of the century 50% of our elderly population will be 75 or older. We face a widening gap between the affluent and the poor, especially the elderly poor—a gap that increased greatly during the 1980s. Already the United States has more poor than other industrialized countries with lower average incomes.

Dramatic changes in family structure have increased the economic vulnerability of many families, with growing implications for social welfare policies. More mothers are working, some at more than one job; the divorce rate is growing, and the number of single-parent families is increasing significantly.

At the start of the 1990s, the United States faced mounting economic problems that led to retrenchment in a number of social programs. Federal spending on civilian programs was reduced from 9.9% of GNP in 1980 to 7.6% in 1990; much of the cut was in social programs. President Bush in his inaugural sounded the warning that more cuts might be necessary when he observed that however much we might wish to build a "kinder and gentler America," we had more "will than wallet." Although we started as a debtor nation following the Revolutionary War, for the first time in its modern history the United States entered the 1990s as a debtor nation. Already the spiraling national deficit has become so large that most new social welfare initiatives have low priority on the national agenda. In 1974 the deficit was less than 1% of GNP and during the later 1970s it hovered around 2%; by the mid-1980s it had grown to 5% of GNP. Because expenditures that appear reasonable in a time of ample resources may very well appear irresponsible in a time of tight budgets, the current situation does not bode well for social welfare programs. This changed environment prompted Lawrence Herson (1990) to ask if we might be approaching a zero-sum society in which limited resources will require that every new service or benefit be matched by reductions in an established service or benefit. What will be the priorities, he asks, of a society historically accustomed to growing affluence and a rising standard of living in a time of diminishing resources?

The mounting national debt was only part of the gloomy economic picture as we faced a number of negative indicators regarding our economic future. At the end of World War II, the United States was producing about one half of the world output of goods and services. In 1991 our GNP was still about two and one half times that of our nearest competitor; but in a time of vitality and growth abroad, the United States found itself mired in stagnation, inactivity, and lagging productivity at home. With increasing global competition, U.S. competitiveness was slipping. Capital investment, which is vital to productivity and economic expansion, was lagging. According to the Washington-based Council on Competitiveness, since 1972 Japan averaged spending 17% of its Gross Domestic Product (GDP) on capital investment, whereas the United States averaged only 12% (*Courier-Journal,* August 16, 1990, p. A-11). The *New York Times* reported that in 1989 the United States invested $513 billion in plant and equipment, whereas the Japanese invested $549 billion ("America's English disease," 1990). And although the U.S. government spends about $60 billion annually on research and development (R&D), this money goes largely to defense, space, and health, with virtually none going for business and commerce. Another factor contributing to the lack of investment resources is the low rate of savings among Americans. During the 1980s Americans went on a consumption binge. In this period net private savings fell to less than one half of what they were during the previous three decades, and even the earlier rate was not all that great compared to some other industrialized countries. These reduced savings rates slowed economic growth and productivity, increasing borrowing abroad and thereby contributing to the growing indebtedness and rising interest payments. Yet another cause for concern is our lagging productivity. Throughout the decades of the 1950s and 1960s, U.S. productivity grew by about 2.5% per year. For the 1970s the rate dropped to about 1.2% annually, and during the 1980s rose again slightly to about 1.6% per year. Beginning in 1989 the rate began to slip downward again, declining 0.7% in 1989, 0.8% in 1990 and about 1.0% in 1991 (Ball, 1991; "Productive u-turn," 1991). These productivity rates are rather low when compared to other industrial countries such as Germany and Japan. Growth in productivity is essential for improving the standard of living without inflation and maintaining the competitiveness of U.S. goods in international markets.

A growing number of studies have pointed up another trend that is also cause for concern. During the 1980s, the United States experienced a decline in higher-paying manufacturing jobs and a shift to lower-paying jobs in the service sector. This trend contributed further to the growth in income inequality noted earlier. In his (1990) book *Our Country,* Michael Barone wrote that federal initiatives such as the GI Bill and the Federal Housing Administration enabled millions of Americans in the years following World War II to move upward socially and economically. Such efforts created a revolutionary expansion of the middle class, he says. In 1991 the middle class was still there, but as a result of economic trends its members were becoming less able to afford what in the past was perceived as the middle-class life-style. As they experienced this decline in life-style, middle-class Americans reacted negatively to paying taxes to provide programs for those less fortunate.

As the country encountered increasing global economic competition, shifted from higher-paying jobs to lesser-paying jobs, and faced a declining standard of living, it became increasingly difficult for citizens and their government to respond positively to the problems of the poor, the homeless, the elderly, and the growing economic underclass in our society.

Some observers disagree that our major problems are economic and contend that attitudes and the absence of strong leadership and a sense of direction are the major stumbling blocks for new initiatives in social welfare policy. Thomas Mann (1990) pointed out that ideas can be a powerful force in policy-making, but only when elite opinion converges around them. Although most Americans can agree on the extent of current social problems, he wrote, there is nothing approaching consensus on how to address these issues in specific public policies.

Public policies are usually reactive rather than proactive, and in the absence of any clear expression of public sentiment on a given issue, policymakers are likely to remain inactive. At the onset of the 1990s the public mood in the United States was marked by considerable ambiguity and lack of clarity. The historian Arthur M. Schlesinger, Jr. (1986), wrote that people tend to be shaped by the events and ideas dominant at the time they reached political awareness (p. 23). The older generation of Americans, shaped by the Great Depression, World War II, and the postwar expansion, see government as a positive force, but many of the younger generation do not share that confidence in government. Some go so far as to question whether U.S. political institutions are any longer capable of solving the complex problems we face. But at the same time they are dissatisfied with their government and many of its efforts, they are unclear in their own minds as to exactly what is needed. Consequently, public discourse is a Tower of Babel offering little or nothing in the way of real solutions for coming to grips with the social issues facing our society.

In such a setting, political leaders often have a tendency to shy away from the tough decisions on complex and difficult issues. In 1991 President Bush and the Congress presided over a nation that was confused and highly fragmented by the host of complex issues faced, and because no consensus existed, both were hesitant to try to initiate potentially controversial actions. As Henry Aaron (1990) noted, "In the absence of national leadership, the United States is avoiding national priorities rather than setting them, jeopardizing future success at home and abroad" (p. 3).

Social Welfare in the Future

Is the impasse of the early 1990s likely to be broken? Many failures in policy-making can be overcome by changes in the conditions that define the problem. In 1991 the population and the economy were undergoing substantial changes and social welfare policies needed overhauling to accommodate these new developments. In the future policymakers will need to address the question of whether the social welfare system, as it has been structured, can meet the needs of our changed society or whether fundamental changes are in order.

Some observers see the major obstacle to new social initiatives not as lack of economic resources but lack of political will. They contend that what is needed are bold, innovative leaders who can redefine the way the general public and its opinion leaders think about these issues. Mann (1990) believed that such leadership is most likely to appear at the state and local levels: "If a renaissance in social policy is to occur under present political conditions, it will almost certainly be led by governors and mayors, not presidents" (p. 314). Others feel that the prospects for change will improve as we move toward the 21st century. Sar A. Levitan, director of the Center for Social Policy at George Washington University, noted: "From 1935 to 1978, we expanded the concept that we were our brothers' and sisters' keepers. In the era of inflation we cut back, but the Reagan era was an aberration. In the 1990s we will expand the concept again" (Kosterlitz, 1988a, p. 999). Schlesinger (1986) believed that periods of governmental activism follow a cyclical pattern and in due time the citizens and leaders again develop a sense of concern and urgency for responding to unmet social needs. According to Schlesinger, the early 1990s should bring a sharp change in the national mood as many Americans discard their indifference toward national politics for more active involvement. This should result in more attention to social policy issues and lead to their elevation on the national agenda.

Conclusion

National social welfare policies came later to the United States than to other industrial Western nations. But once in place these programs

Table 1.1 Government Spending on Social Programs 1960-1987

Year	Total (billions of dollars)	Annual percentage change[a]	Percent of: Total GNP[b]	Percent of: Total outlays
Total Expenditures				
1960	52.3	8.3	10.3	38.4
1970	145.9	10.8	14.7	48.2
1975	290.1	14.7	19.0	57.3
1980	492.5	11.2	18.5	56.5
1985	737.2	8.4	18.4	52.3
1986	782.8	6.2	18.5	52.2
1987	834.4	6.6	18.4	53.5
Federal Expenditures				
1960	25.0	9.0	4.9	28.1
1970	77.3	12.0	7.8	40.1
1975	167.4	16.7	11.0	52.0
1980	302.6	12.6	11.3	54.3
1985	453.0	8.4	11.3	48.6
1986	472.0	4.2	11.2	48.3
1987	499.8	5.9	11.0	50.4
State and Local Government Expenditures				
1960	27.3	7.7	5.4	60.1
1970	68.5	9.6	6.9	64.0
1975	122.7	12.4	8.0	65.3
1980	189.9	9.1	7.1	60.8
1985	284.1	8.4	7.1	60.5
1986	310.8	9.4	7.3	60.4
1987	334.6	7.7	7.4	59.6

a. Change from prior year shown; for 1960, change from 1950.
b. Gross national product.
SOURCE: U.S. Social Security Administration, Social Security Bulletin, November 1989.

expanded enormously, and in spite of considerable ambivalence on the issue, most Americans have come to expect the government to assume an increasingly broader role in providing social services. Despite the enormous growth over the last half century, the U.S. welfare state is still less extensive than that of most Western democracies, and the United States spends a smaller portion of its GNP on such services than do most West European governments. About 55%-60% of federal spending currently goes to social programs (Chisman & Pifer, 1987, p. 59; see Table 1.1).

Although social programs come in for more than their share of challenges and criticism, most observers do not see much likelihood of their abandonment. Whatever shortcomings they may perceive, most Americans do not want social welfare programs dismantled entirely. Politicians who have proposed eliminating or overhauling major aspects of these programs have not fared well with the voters. The Reagan "revolution" produced some modest changes and reductions in social welfare policy, but no public assistance programs were abolished during Reagan's administration. In fact, Reagan probably encountered more opposition and criticism for his social welfare initiatives than in any other area. Though they may complain about their high tax rates, most Americans accept the government's role in promoting the general welfare. Public opinion polls show continued support for social programs and even support for extensions of such services in certain areas (Chisman & Pifer, 1987; Ford Foundation, 1989b). The dissatisfactions expressed by many people were apparently not so much with the programs and their underlying goals and purposes as with the agencies and leaders who failed to make them work as intended. People do make some distinctions among programs, however. Social insurance programs (social security, medicare, unemployment insurance) are more generally accepted; assistance programs (AFDC, medicaid) are more controversial. Many people still harbor strong resentment toward supporting those who they feel are capable of making their own living. The former programs are viewed to be public aid as a matter of right, whereas the latter are public aid as a matter of sufferance.

As these programs undergo close scrutiny during the next decade, shifts in emphasis will no doubt occur and various reforms will be undertaken to make these programs more "effective," but it is unlikely that any massive reversals will come in the near future. A primary reason for this is that over time these programs have developed a vast constituency that is quite protective of its interests. The Census Bureau estimates that about one half of all households in the United States received some form of benefit from the welfare state (Chisman & Pifer, 1987, p. 66). A 1986 survey by the bureau showed that over a 32-month period almost one in five Americans received some type of welfare benefit for at least as long as 1 month. Another potent political element is the fact that many who benefit from these programs, such as farmers and merchants, whose sales are expanded by food stamps, and builders, developers, and financial institutions, who profit from housing construction, are members of the middle class and are more politically active and influential than the poor. Thus even though presidents and the Congress may seek some reforms or changes in direction in the social welfare programs, they won't seriously consider dismantling, because they realize such an effort would amount to political suicide.

Debate over social welfare policy will continue to be influenced by a number of conflicting factors. As noted earlier, Americans tend to be highly ambivalent on these issues: ideologically they are conservatives, operationally they are liberals (see Chisman & Pifer, 1987). In his (1990) book *Social Welfare,* Dobelstein observed: "Social welfare policies in particular seem to evoke the most acrimonious debates over what kind of information is relevant to policy choices" (p. ix). On such issues, the policymakers ultimately are influenced more by their perceptions of constituent needs and desires than by research findings. Although social policies experienced several years of growth relatively free of economic policy issues, the unprecedented rise in the national deficit during the 1980s forced the debate of the 1990s back into that arena. In light of the trends and circumstances of the early 1990s, debate on social policy issues will be ideological, economic, political, and heated for some time to come.

Note

1. From "Programs Worth Saving" by Thomas Eagleton, *The Atlantic, July 1982,* pp. 8ff. Reprinted with permission.

2

Reducing Poverty's Sting

With our nation's strong capitalist, individualist tradition, one of the most controversial aspects of social welfare policies in the United States has been the redistribution of income. As a part of this tradition many still feel strongly that persons who persevere and are willing to work hard should be able to earn their own way. Nevertheless, the fact remains that U.S. society is one of extreme contrasts economically. Although our capitalistic system is unequaled in its productivity, it is not without its shortcomings. The United States as a whole is one of the world's most affluent societies, but a substantial portion of its citizens face a bleak existence on the fringes of that affluence. At the same time that our nation and many of its citizens are richer than ever before, poverty remains a painful fact of life for a significant portion of our population.

Current estimates put the number of Americans living in poverty at somewhat over 30 million (see Figure 2.1 and Table 2.1). The official poverty level for a family of four in 1990 was $12,675, and 13.5% of the population fell below that level (U.S. Bureau of the Census, 1990, p. 458). Much of the poverty in the United States exists in several hard-core pockets of the population. Poverty rates are quite unequal among different segments of society. About 70% of those living in poverty lived in large metropolitan areas, but the rate of poverty was higher in rural areas, where in 1987 more than one of every six persons

Table 2.1 Persons Below Poverty Level

Category	Persons Below Poverty Level (millions)							Percent Below Poverty Level						
	1960	1970	1980	1985	1986	1987	1988	1960	1970	1980	1985	1986	1987	1988
All Persons	39.9	25.4	29.3	33.1	32.4	32.8	31.7	22.2	12.6	13.0	14.0	13.6	13.5	13.0
White	28.3	17.5	19.7	22.9	22.2	21.4	20.7	17.8	9.9	10.2	11.4	11.0	10.5	10.1
Black	NA	7.5	8.6	8.9	9.0	9.7	9.4	NA	33.5	32.5	31.3	31.1	31.1	31.3
Hispanic	NA	NA	NA	5.1	5.5	5.4	NA	NA	NA	25.7	NA	27.3	28.2	26.7
Single-Parent Female Head House-holds	NA	NA	NA	16.4	16.9	16.9	NA	NA	NA	NA	41.9	41.1	42.4	NA

SOURCES: *World Almanac* (1990, p. 651); U.S. Bureau of the Census (1990, Table No. 744, p. 459).

lived in poverty. The young and the elderly experience higher rates of poverty than the population generally, although the poverty rate for the elderly has been reduced significantly. In the 1950s the elderly experienced poverty rates of 35%; but with the elderly becoming the primary beneficiaries of federal social spending these rates have been sharply reduced. In fact, some see the reduction of poverty among the elderly as one of the biggest social welfare success stories. This reduction in poverty among the elderly can be misleading, however; 20% of the elderly are less than 25% above the poverty line and almost 30% of those not in poverty are within $5,000 of the poverty line. Put another way, 20.9% of the elderly are near poor compared to 18.7% for the general population, placing the elderly at higher risk for falling into poverty. The elderly still have the highest poverty rate of all adult Americans; only children under 18 years of age have a higher rate (Pollack, 1990).

Next to the elderly, children are the principal beneficiaries of social welfare spending. Thirty percent of children under age six get benefits and 27% of those under age 18 get some benefits. But poverty rates among children are quite high. Among children under 10 years of age the rate in the 1980s was over 20% and for children under 5 years it was even higher (Eskey, 1990; U.S. Congress, House Select Committee on Children, Youth and Families, 1989). Many observers fear that youngsters growing up in such an environment have only the slightest of chances of breaking the cycle of poverty and succeeding in life.

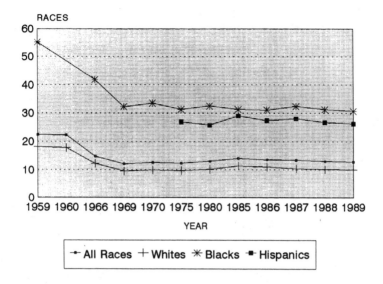

Figure 2.1. Persons Below the Poverty Level, 1959 to 1989
SOURCE: *Statistical Abstract of the U.S., 1991,* 111th ed., Table #745, p. 462.

Minorities also tend to experience poverty in disproportionate numbers. Although 48% of those living in poverty are white, poverty rates among blacks and Hispanics are considerably higher than for the population generally. In 1988 the overall poverty rate was 13% while the rate for blacks was 31.6% and that of Hispanics was 26.8% (*World Almanac and Book of Facts,* 1990, p. 561; see Figure 2.1).

One of the factors complicating the poverty problem is the capitalist system's uneven distribution of income and economic benefits across society. In 1991 the inequality of family incomes in the United States was greater than 20 or 30 years ago. In fact, the gap between the rich and the poor was at its greatest point since the 1940s (see Tables 2.2 and 2.3). Inequality of incomes has grown for the last 20 years. Economic recessions always tend to hit the poor and near poor hardest, thus increasing income inequality among the rich and poor. So with income growth slowing dramatically in the 1970s and early 1980s, the average poor person fell further behind economically. The economic recovery of the mid-1980s failed to follow the usual pattern, and the average poor

Table 2.2 Growing Inequality in U.S. Incomes, 1969-1989

Year	Percentage of Income Received by Each Quintile 1969-1989				
	Lowest	Second	Middle	Fourth	Highest
1969	5.6	12.4	17.7	23.7	40.6
1974	5.5	12.0	17.5	24.0	41.0
1979	5.2	11.6	17.5	24.1	41.7
1980	5.1	11.6	17.5	24.3	41.6
1981	5.0	11.3	17.4	24.4	41.9
1982	4.7	11.2	17.1	24.3	42.7
1983	4.7	11.1	17.1	24.3	42.8
1984	4.7	11.0	17.0	24.4	42.9
1985	4.6	10.0	16.9	24.2	43.5
1986	4.6	10.8	16.8	24.0	43.7
1987	4.6	10.8	16.9	24.1	43.7
1988	4.6	10.7	16.7	24.0	44.0
1989	4.6	10.6	16.5	23.7	44.6

Range of Quintiles in 1988
  Lowest: Under $15,102
  Second: $15,102-26,182
  Middle: $26,182-38,500
  Fourth: $38,500-55,906
  Highest: Over $55,906

SOURCE: U.S. Bureau of the Census (1990).

person continued to fall even further behind. Incomes at all levels experienced some growth, but those of the rich grew much faster.

In 1969 the wealthiest one fifth of U.S. households received 43% of total income; by 1979 their share was 44.2%; and by 1989 it had reached 46.8%. Those at the bottom of the scale received smaller and smaller shares. From 1983 to 1987 the share of the bottom one fifth declined from 5.6% to 4.3%. Of considerable concern, as they pay the major share of taxes, was the share of the middle class. The share of the middle 20% of the population dropped to 16.7% in 1988 from a high of 18.1% in 1957. This decline meant their share of all income was at its lowest in over 40 years ("Income gap between U.S. rich, poor widened in Reagan years," 1990; Kaus, 1990).

Because of the nature of our system, political decisions often tend to exacerbate these shortcomings in the economic system rather than alleviate them. The 1986 Tax Reform Act, for example, contributed to the widening gap between the rich and the poor. According to the

Table 2.3 Family Income

| Type of Family | Number (1000) | | | | Median Income (Dollars) | | | |
	All Families	White	Black	Hispanic	All Families	White	Black	Hispanic
Married Couple Family	52,100	46,877	3,722	3,398	36,389	36,840	30,385	25,667
wife working	29,713	26,402	2,414	1,766	42,709	43,182	36,709	31,864
wife not working	22,387	20,475	1,308	1,632	27,220	27,958	18,515	19,117
Single Parent Family								
male householder	2,847	2,274	464	314	26,827	28,935	17,853	21,937
female householder	10,890	7,342	3,223	1,112	15,346	17,672	10,657	10,687
Number of Wage Earners in Family								
None	9,438	7,820	1,364	622	13,729	15,552	6,108	6,545
One	18,189	15,107	2,573	1,588	23,872	25,993	14,006	15,841
Two	28,984	25,513	2,654	1,891	38,702	39,413	31,875	28,401
Three	6,680	5,798	639	530	48,977	49,927	42,002	36,897
Four or more	2,546	2,255	179	213	67,920	65,853	53,635	49,138
All Families	65,837	56,492	7,409	4,823	32,915	39,915	19,329	21,769

SOURCE: U.S. Bureau of the Census, Current Population Reports, Series p-60, No. 166, *The Statistical Abstract of the United States, 1990,* 110th ed. (Washington, D.C., 1990), p. 451.

Heritage Foundation, the tax burden for a family of four has risen from 2% of income in 1948 to 24% in 1988 (*Conference on the Trend,* 1976; "Income Gap," 1990; Kaus, 1990; Reich, 1991).

Wealthy households, however, paid a smaller percentage of their income in taxes in 1990 than they did in 1980. Consequently, most affluent Americans gained income during the 1980s, middle-income people gained only slightly, and lower-income persons lost ground. From 1980 to 1990 households in the top one fifth in incomes gained about 33%; the middle one fifth gained about 3%; and the poorest one fifth lost about 5%. These patterns of income distribution result in the richest 1% of the population receiving as much income as the total for the bottom 40%. In 1990 the bottom 40% earned 14.2% of total income while the top 1% accounted for 12.6% of total national income. In 1980 the top 1% received only about half as much of total income as the lower

40% after taxes. Because percentages can give a somewhat incomplete picture, let us put this another way. From 1980 to 1988 the richest 10% of the population received about a $16,000 increase in after-tax income whereas those families at the low end of the scale lost about $1,000 in income, a sizeable figure if total income is $10,000 or less to begin with. From 1980 to 1990, the wealthiest 1% of the population gained $214,000 to $400,000 on their incomes. Much of this increase for the wealthy resulted from capital gains on which President Bush proposed to give the already rich an even greater tax advantage. Approximately 66% of the benefits from a reduction in the capital gains tax would go to those who already have incomes of $100,000 or more per year (Kaus, 1990; Reich, 1991).

In 1966 pollsters reported that 45% of Americans said they saw the United States as a place where the "rich get richer and the poor get poorer." In the late 1980s 81% of those polled agreed with that perception (Ford Foundation, 1989b, p. 5). Why then does the political process continue to produce decisions that further contribute to these disparities? A major reason is that our system tends to be most responsive to those elements that are most politically active and command the most political resources. Unfortunately those who need the government's help the most are the ones most likely to fall through the cracks in such a political system.

Lacking a strong political voice, the poor in our society tend to be easily overlooked or ignored. In a way, they are also a paradox, existing in the easily missed corners of the wealthiest society the world has ever known. Writing in the mid-1960s, Ben Bagdikian observed, the poor live "in the midst of plenty"; they are occupying "a world inside our society in which the American dream is dying" (1964, pp. 6-7). It was Michael Harrington, in his book *The Other America* (1962), who really brought the plight of the poor to Americans' attention in the 1960s. Describing what he called "the strangest poor in the history of mankind," because they existed in the midst of affluence, Harrington said the poor in the United States were largely invisible. "The American poor," he wrote, "are pessimistic and defeated and they are victimized by mental suffering to a degree unknown in Suburbia." "Here," Harrington continued, "are the unskilled workers, the migrant farm workers, the aged, the minorities, and all the others who live in the economic underworld of American life" (p. 650). With Harrington championing their cause, the poor gained a degree of public attention and *The Other America* provided the intellectual underpinnings for President Johnson's War on Poverty.

The War on Poverty

Following his election in 1960, John F. Kennedy put forward an ambitious agenda of social initiatives, most of which stalled in Congress. But a growing sentiment that poverty in the midst of plenty was unacceptable and JFK's assassination paved the way for President Johnson's call for action. In March 1964, Johnson told Congress, "I have called for a national war on poverty. Our objective," he continued, "is total victory." Later, when signing the Economic Opportunity Act of 1964, the president announced that it was now the objective of the United States to afford the poor that degree of security that would enable them to "move with the majority along the high road of hope and prosperity."

The War on Poverty was conceived as a broad-based, multifaceted assault on poverty from several fronts. Toward these ends, President Johnson asked Congress for action on a broad range of legislative proposals, including:

1. Appalachian development
2. Youth employment (Job Corps, Neighborhood Youth Corps)
3. Expanded food stamp distribution
4. A national service corps (VISTA)
5. More stable unemployment insurance benefits
6. Extension of coverage under the minimum wage
7. Expanded federal aid to education in poorer communities (ESEA)
8. Construction of more hospitals and libraries
9. Hospital insurance for the aged (Medicare)
10. Expanded public housing
11. Federal aid for mass transit to help the urban poor

Though he did not get everything he asked for, Johnson's efforts greatly expanded the federal government's social welfare role and touched off a debate on such issues that continues into the current decade.

A major thrust of several of the programs in the War on Poverty was to provide the poor with education and job training that would enable particularly the young to compete more effectively. Among these efforts were:

Head Start designed to provide prekindergarten schooling to children from educationally deprived backgrounds so they would be better prepared to begin their formal schooling.

Upward Bound was to identify bright but underachieving high school students from low-income families and prepare them for and encourage them toward higher education, usually through participation in summer programs on college/university campuses.

Neighborhood Youth Corps provided federal assistance to state and local governments for programs to hire teenagers from low-income backgrounds for part-time and summer community projects with the objectives of providing work experience and income and reducing the pressures on such youths to drop out of school before graduating to seek full-time work.

Job Corps was designed to remove high school age youths having problems from the potentially corrupting and distracting influences of their homes and neighborhoods and provide them with 2 years of education and job training in basic skills centers.

Whereas these efforts focused primarily on changing the personal traits and attitudes of poor youths, two other programs were directed more toward some restructuring of social institutions and practices to help the poor gain better access to jobs, goods, services, and the political process.

Legal Services was designed to ensure the poor were not denied the rights due them simply because they could not afford the legal costs. One of the more controversial elements of the War on Poverty package was the Community Action Agency requirement. This provision sought to provide a decision-making role for the poor by requiring the establishment of local Community Action agencies that included representatives from the poor residents of the area. These agencies were to coordinate and oversee the delivery of services in their neighborhoods, make decisions on the mix and style of programs undertaken, and provide a sense of involvement and commitment for the community.

Other legislative elements of the overall effort included Volunteers in Service to America (VISTA), a domestic version of the Peace Corps that sent volunteers into poor communities to provide a variety of services and assistance; the Elementary and Secondary Education Act, which extended federal assistance to children from economically disadvantaged families; the Medicare and medicaid programs; and expansion of the school lunch and food stamp programs. The overall emphasis of the programs was mainly that of equalizing opportunity so that the poor could compete more equally with others in the private sector.

Like the Vietnam War, the War on Poverty quickly became the object of persistent controversy. Its critics tended to write it off as a massive and costly government intervention in social programming that failed dismally. Because perceptions growing out of these expansive efforts of the 1960s continue to have such a significant influence on debates over social policy, it becomes important to get some understanding of what the War on Poverty was and was not.

In several respects the War on Poverty was a contradiction in that its structure and implementation conflicted with its overall philosophy and objectives. Philosophically the War on Poverty was based on the idea that poverty stems from the institutions of society and people's environmental circumstances and therefore is more structural than cultural or individual. It is not necessarily natural and inevitable, but can be addressed and alleviated, if not eliminated, through appropriate social policies. By altering those social and economic conditions that cause poverty, the cycle can be broken and those caught in its bonds can be set free.

In its enactment and implementation, the War on Poverty actually reflected very little of this philosophy. In the end its primary thrust was to change the poor to fit the existing system rather than seeking to change the system. For example, in the job training components, one of its major efforts, the assumption was that once the necessary skills were acquired, the private sector would be waiting ready, willing, and able to provide ample-paying jobs for all those trained. The plan included no element aimed at changing the system to guarantee jobs for those trained.

To really understand the War on Poverty it is necessary to sort through all the rhetoric both pro and con and look at what actually occurred. President Johnson and his supporters launched the program by implying a much broader and more coordinated effort than was ever forthcoming. The program did involve a variety of efforts, but as Jeffrey Henig noted, a multiplicity of tactics should not be confused with breadth and depth of commitment (Henig, 1985, p. 102; see also Haveman, 1987). Theodore Lowi (1979) questioned the degree of real commitment, noting that all the War on Poverty measures represented only about $0.5 billion in new dollars whereas the Vietnam War commanded over $2 billion in new expenditures (p. 211). Nor did the multifaceted approach easily translate into a cohesive, coordinated policy. To broaden the base of political support and pull in the votes needed in Congress, something was included for virtually every relevant and potentially helpful constituent interest. These efforts to broaden the base of political support came at the sacrifice of a more focused, coherent, and consistent approach.

Despite the almost total absence of any provisions directed toward systemic changes, many of its critics branded the War on Poverty as a misguided effort by the national government to solve what should largely remain state and local issues. Some critics also contended that the War on Poverty reflected a distrust of the private sector and a naive faith in the national government's ability to solve social problems. Little in the actual implementation and functioning of the program appears to support such charges. In a few localities the Community Action agencies did challenge existing political structures and did bring some new elements into the decision-making process, but overall the programs were more federal in name and funding than in their actual administration. On the whole, implementation was quite decentralized and the states were allowed considerable discretion in virtually all the programs. Several states actually became concerned that the programs were too decentralized—to the point that they were being bypassed and decision making was too much in the hands of the low-income residents in local communities (Henig, 1985, pp. 86-126).

In the final analysis much of the criticism leveled at the War on Poverty is based on misconception rather than the facts reflected by welfare statistics. Most welfare recipients are not minorities, but are whites. Most welfare recipients really are not able to work—most are children—and most of the adult recipients are elderly or disabled. Welfare families are not unusually large. In fact, over 40% have only one child and another 28% have only two. Despite the widespread concept of a large "welfare class," many who are eligible to receive assistance are not enrolled. Only about 40% of those eligible actually receive food stamps, and of those eligible for supplemental security income 55% are receiving benefits (Bagdikian, 1964; Chisman & Pifer, 1987; Henig, 1985; Schwartz, 1988). In spite of the facts, myths about social welfare are widespread and persistent. During the two decades following their enactment, these programs did help to reduce poverty levels in the United States (see Figure 2.1 and Table 2.1). But like the Vietnam War, the War on Poverty was constantly beleaguered by doubters and critics on many fronts.

Efforts at Solution

The cornerstone for federal income maintenance efforts is the Social Security Act adopted by Congress in 1935 as a part of President Franklin

**Billions
of Dollars**

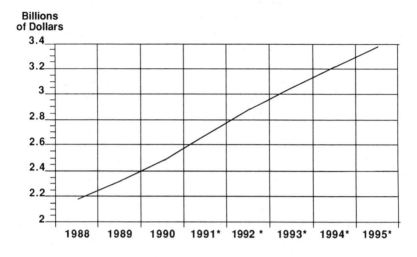

Figure 2.2. Social Security Outlays, 1988-1995
*Estimated
SOURCE: Budget of the United States.

Roosevelt's New Deal program. Today 68% of federal income maintenance funds are distributed through various benefits provided under social security. These services have become the largest domestic spending program, consuming about 20% of the national budget. (See Figure 2.2 on growth in social security outlays.)

What is commonly called social security is really a package of several programs providing a variety of benefits to different categories of eligible persons. Overall the program incorporates two basic concepts or approaches—social insurance programs that are based on participants' contributions and social assistance programs that are noncontributory.

The social insurance or contributory programs are financed through a system of employee and employer taxes. In his original plan, FDR proposed to fund social security out of general fund revenues, but congressional Republicans and Southern Democrats forced him to accept the more regressive payroll tax approach. Consequently, lower- and middle-class workers feel the bite of these taxes most. Also the elements pushing the contributory approach insisted that benefits be tied to contributions so that social security would not be primarily a redistributive program. Therefore, social security today is only mildly redistributive, making some transfers from wealthier earners to poorer and younger to older.

The contributory programs were a forced savings plan under which employees and employers were required to pay matching amounts into a benefits fund. In 1937 the tax was 1% on the first $3,000 in wages and remained at that level until 1950; since then Congress has increased the rates to meet rising costs of the program and the rate currently is 7.65% on the first $51,300 earned (See Table 2.3). As originally conceived, social security was a pay-as-you-go plan in which contributions by current workers were used to pay the benefits of those already retired. But as benefits were increased and the worker/retiree ratio declined over the years, by the 1970s the system was faced with shortfalls and critics began to question its solvency. In 1976, for example, the trust fund took in $72.3 billion but paid out $78 billion.

Changes offered by two study commissions for reforming the system were adopted by Congress. The most recent changes, adopted in 1983 as a result of the Greenspan commission's recommendations, have resulted in the accumulation of large reserves in the trust fund. Some observers project the reserve will hit $2 trillion shortly after the turn of the century. The purpose of this reserve was to meet the increased benefits demands when the so-called baby boom generation reaches retirement age. When this occurs the ratio of retirees to current workers paying into the system will rise dramatically, and without a large reserve, the fund could not withstand the drain. But some fear that with our current deficit problems these funds will be tapped for other purposes and will no longer be available when needed by future retirees. They point out that the large baby boom generation that has been asked to make larger contributions to meet the demands they would later generate may encounter a situation where their own benefits are in jeopardy.

At the present time the reserve is being deposited in government securities. If this continues, by the year 2010 the social security system will own a large part of the national debt. Some observers see potential risks with this surplus accumulation. Senator Daniel Moynihan (D., NY) proposed reducing the payroll tax to reduce the excess income into the fund, but his plan was not embraced in Congress. Some feel it would be better to keep the system on a pay-as-you-go basis; otherwise, they fear, the temptation to liberalize benefits or use the surplus for other purposes may prove too great. Paul C. Light (1985) wrote:

> If you leave the Social Security trust fund alone over the next ten years,
> there's no way the government is not going to spend it. It's a lot of money.
> It's a tax that's already in place, you don't have to do anything to use it.
> I don't expect to see it accumulate and be held in sacred trust. (p. 363)

When signing the Social Security Act into law on August 14, 1935, President Roosevelt observed that the legislation was only the "cornerstone in a structure which is being built but is by no means complete." The original act provided only Old Age and Survivor's Insurance (OASI) and Aid for the Aged. Today the program has been expanded to cover millions more so that approximately 90% of workers are now covered. The only workers who do not contribute to social security are state and local employees who participate in comparable state or local programs. In 1939 Congress extended coverage under the program to spouses and surviving dependents of those who had contributed to the program. In 1956 insurance covering those who became disabled on the job or their dependents was added, and in 1965 Medicare was added. From its modest beginnings, the program has grown to one providing a wide range of benefits to millions of Americans (see Tables 2.4 and 2.5).

Retirement Insurance

The largest program and the one to which most people are referring when they speak of social security is the program of retirement insurance provided under Title II of the Social Security Act of 1935. This is a comprehensive income maintenance program for workers and their families, providing benefits for retired workers, disabled workers and their dependents, spouses of retired workers, children, widows and widowers, and parents of workers. This program is designed to provide eligible workers with replacement income when they retire. To qualify, a worker must contribute to the system for 5 years, rising to 10 years by 1991. Benefits upon retirement are based on the level of earnings over a period of years, and persons can retire at age 65 and draw full benefits or at age 62 with 80% benefits. Under the 1983 reforms the age for receiving full benefits will be raised gradually to age 67 in 2003. Since social security is a substitute for earnings lost as a result of retirement, there is a penalty for those who continue to work if they earn above certain amounts. In 1991 recipients could earn up to $8,400 without penalty. After that threshold was reached, benefits were reduced

$1 for every $3 earned. Those who postpone retirement to age 70 are awarded credits that avoid this penalty. Also since the 1983 changes, one half the benefits of retirees who have incomes above $25,000 (single) or $32,000 (couples) are taxable. Benefits of those below these levels are not taxed.

Social security was not conceived as a program providing full retirement, but as a supplemental income replacement source. Many Americans are dependent on the program as their primary source of income upon retirement, however. A 1987 study by the Social Security Administration revealed that 80% of beneficiaries had no other sources of income. The average income of all recipients was $8,410, only slightly above the official poverty level. Of the 20% studied who had incomes over $20,000, one fifth of their income was from social security. Currently 98% of retired persons collect social security payments and 23% of all families receive some social security benefits (Pollack, 1990).

Social security benefits have improved as a source of replacement income but remain low for those relying on them as their sole source of income. In 1972 social security replaced 38% of a 65-year-old male's preretirement pay. In 1975 Congress approved a system for indexing benefits; that is, when the Consumer Price Index increased more than 3% during the year, beneficiaries would automatically receive cost of living adjustments (COLAs) in their payments. Under this approach, beneficiaries have received annual cost of living increases each year since 1975 except for 6 months in 1983 when adjustments were deferred because the social security fund was facing a possible deficit (see Table 2.6). By 1977 benefits had risen to 45% of preretirement income and in 1981 reached 54%. Since 1981 benefits have leveled off at about 41% of preretirement income for a 65-year-old male (Kosterlitz, 1989a).

In 1990 the benefit for the average retired worker was $602 per month, or $7,224 per year. The maximum monthly benefit for a worker retiring at age 65 in 1991 was $1,022 per month, or $12,264 per year. Benefits for a disabled worker were $587 per month, or $1,022 per month for a disabled worker with spouse and children. A widow with two children would receive $1,203 per month and an elderly couple with both drawing benefits would receive $1,022 per month. For many recipients payments are quite modest and often not enough taken alone to raise them above the poverty level. For some, social security is less than half their total income, but frequently even the combined total is still less than the poverty level. Although social security has reduced poverty significantly among elderly persons, there remain those for whom it is insufficient.

Unemployment Insurance

The Social Security Act also included federal incentives to the states encouraging them to establish programs of unemployment insurance meeting minimum federal standards. All states now have unemployment insurance programs, but because each state administers its own program, the benefits and coverage vary considerably state to state. Funded by taxes levied on employer payrolls, benefits to those who lose their jobs or are laid off from work are paid by the states in weekly checks. Coverage under the unemployment insurance program is quite spotty and many persons working in part-time, temporary, or low-income jobs are not covered. Only about one half of all employed workers are currently covered and at any particular point only about one third of those who are unemployed are receiving benefits (Ford Foundation, 1989b). Also, most states provide benefits for only limited periods of time, and those who are out of work for extended periods usually exhaust their available benefits before new employment is found. Coverage under the current program is patchwork in nature and benefits are often insufficient to meet the needs of those who are out of work.

Supplemental Security Income

The programs discussed thus far were designed to replace income lost by workers upon retirement or loss of their jobs. The Social Security Act also included provisions addressing the needs of those unable to participate in the contributory programs. In 1972 Aid to the Aged, Aid to the Blind, and Aid to the Disabled were combined under the title of Supplemental Security Income (SSI) and the federal government took over administration from the states. Under the new approach federal benefits are standardized but the states may supplement the level of support provided if they so desire. The maximum federal payment under SSI for 1991 is $407 per month for an individual and $610 per month for a couple. About one third of the states currently supplement these federally guaranteed amounts. Adequacy of income is still a problem for some, as SSI benefits alone can be as low as 76% of the official poverty level. Because social security and SSI overlap, well over one half of SSI recipients also draw benefits under social security; as SSI is a needs-based program and social security benefits are regarded as income, SSI payments are reduced accordingly. As a consequence, some lose virtually all of their SSI benefits as a result of benefits under social security retirement. About 4.5 million persons receive benefits under SSI, almost two thirds of whom are disabled workers eligible for some coverage under social security retirement.

Aid for Dependent Children

The other major social assistance program under the Social Security Act was the Aid to Families With Dependent Children program (AFDC). Unlike the contributory or so-called entitlement programs, SSI and AFDC are "means tested." This requires applicants for benefits under these programs to show a definite need for assistance and a lack of the ability to provide it themselves. Benefits are provided, not as a matter of right, but on the basis of demonstrated need. AFDC also is a joint federal-state program and as a consequence benefit levels vary substantially. In 1989 almost 4 million families received benefits under AFDC, with the average being $381 per month. The high was $615 per month in Alaska and the low $113 per month in Alabama (*World Almanac,* 1990, p. 562). AFDC will be discussed in more detail in Chapter 6.

Various other programs either directly or indirectly provide some income assistance to selected segments of the population. One of the oldest forms of income support was for veterans who had fought in wars on behalf of the country. As recently as 1912, it was estimated that over two thirds of all white males in the North who were 65 or older received pensions from the federal government (Chisman & Pifer, 1987, p. 38). The current veterans' pension program dates from 1933 and provides benefits for needy wartime veterans age 65 or older who are permanently and totally disabled, but not from war-related service. The income tax code provides some income maintenance for select groups such as the blind and the poor. Those whose income is below a certain level may qualify for an income tax credit. On the whole the tax laws tend to provide the greatest benefits to those needing them least.

A variety of benefits of a more indirect nature are also available, but because of their lack of focus and coherence and the stigma often attached to them, these programs have generally been less efficient than the more direct cash benefits efforts. These noncash or in-kind benefits have been greatly expanded since 1965. From 1965 to 1984 cash benefits grew by 56% whereas for the same period in-kind benefits mushroomed by 800%. Some of these programs, however, have been around for some time. The **food stamp program** usually associated with the 1960s actually has roots going back to 1939. The modern version has been extended to provide benefits to 20 million poor families. Dating from 1946 the **National School Lunch Program** provides lunches for children from nursery school through high school. Under the program children from needy families receive free meals; those from less needy families receive meals at reduced prices. The **Women, Infants and Children (WIC) program** provides supplemental feeding benefits for pregnant women, infants, and children. At the other end of the spectrum, over 200 million meals are provided annually for the elderly under the **Older Americans Act of 1965.**

Because they are more indirect efforts at reducing poverty and its effects, in-kind programs are based on a different premise. Cash benefits are based on the idea that what poor people need is money; proponents of the in-kind programs maintain that higher levels of benefits can be provided through this approach, giving recipients an overall higher standard of living than would be possible using cash benefits alone. Critics of in-kind programs attack the approach as paternalistic and charge that it denies recipients the freedom and responsibility to manage their resources and lives according to their own desires. Several of these programs will be examined in more detail in succeeding chapters.

Conclusion

Adoption of the Social Security Act in 1935 signaled the recognition of the federal government's responsibility for undertaking programs to protect the welfare of its citizens. These programs have provided the core for a social welfare system that has expanded dramatically from these beginnings. Through the years Congress has enacted a variety of social policies that have moderately redistributed wealth from higher to lower income persons; from younger, working persons to older, retired persons; from employers to employees. The ultimate purpose of such undertakings has been to promote the general well-being of the American people, but these efforts have not been accomplished without considerable political controversy and debate.

Without a doubt the most efficient and most effective of the national government's antipoverty programs has been the social security retirement insurance program; yet, this program remains quite controversial and illustrates the ongoing debate surrounding such social welfare efforts. Since 1940 the administrative costs of this program have held steady at about 1.2% of total expenditures and benefits from the program have kept millions of Americans from lives of poverty. Yet, conservative critics have never been happy with the system, challenging both the concept and the fiscal soundness of the approach. They oppose the compulsory contributions and contend persons should have the option of participating in or making contributions to their own retirement plans. Recent trends in the system led to growing criticism and questions as to its actuarial and fiscal soundness. President Reagan's former director of the Office of Management and Budget, James C. Miller III, described social security as a Ponzi scheme that would leave tomorrow's workers holding the bag. The critics challenge the wisdom of transferring large sums from taxes paid by current workers to benefits payments for retired workers. They are especially concerned with this feature because of the declining ratio of workers to retirees. In 1960 the ratio was about five active workers for each retiree; that figure has declined to three workers to each retiree and predictions are that by the middle of the 21st century the ratio will decline further to two workers for each retiree (Eskey, 1990, p. 89). Critics question whether the system can remain solvent under such increasing benefits demands even with its currently accumulating surplus. Phillip Longman, author of *Born to Pay* (1987), says the social security system has come to depend on several broad contingencies, none of which seems very likely as the baby boom generation passes through the system. Unless current trends are soon reversed, he predicted, the baby boomers are headed for a disastrous retirement (Longman, 1985, pp. 73-81).

Adding to the concern of some are the current trends in social welfare spending and changing demographics. At present the elderly comprise about 12% of the population and consume over 30% of the budget and over 50% of social services spending. By the year 2015 those over age 65 will comprise approximately one half of the nation's adult population. Currently the 85 and older group is the fastest growing segment of the U.S. population, which means persons are living longer and drawing more in social security. Those over age 85 presently number about 3 million; this number will hit 8.6 million by 2020 and 17.8 million in 2040 (Schneider & Guralnik, 1990). If our current commitment to the elderly is maintained, this means greatly expanded expenditures on programs for the aged.

Several critics feel the social security retirement program is unfair in a number of respects. Some feel the current approach takes income from those who need it most (the young) and gives it to others who need it less (more affluent elderly). These critics see a growing polarization along economic lines and a potential confrontation between workers and retirees. They also object to the wealthy receiving benefits that they feel are undeserved. Congressman James Moody (D., WI) contended, "It's not fair to spend society's money to preserve assets for someone's children" (Pollack, 1990). Many critics also challenge the ratio of benefits drawn to the taxes paid into the system. High-wage earners will have recouped all the taxes they paid into the system in less than 3 years of retirement. In fact, the average worker who retired in 1988 recovered all his/her taxes within 21 months after retiring (Eskey, 1990, p. 88). Such challenges prompted Senator David Durenberger (R., MN), one of the founders of Americans for Generational Equity, to predict: "The assumption that each working generation will take care of the one that preceded it is finished" (Smith, 1990).

Like predictions of Mark Twain's death, such claims would seem premature, because although support for such welfare programs as AFDC may wax and wane, the social security retirement program appears to have achieved a solid popular political base. Such conservative politicians as Barry Goldwater and Ronald Reagan have learned quickly that you do not suggest drastic changes in this program. In fact, Eskey (1990) wrote: "As a political issue, social security has become so untouchable that proposals to tax benefits or to reduce cost-of-living increases are considered foolhardy on Capitol Hill" (p. 88). This is not difficult to understand when one considers that 98% of all retired people in the United States receive benefits under the program along with a variety of other beneficiaries, and older adults tend to vote in higher proportions than any other age group. Former secretary of the Department of Health, Education and Welfare (now Health and Human Services) Arthur Fleming maintained:

> Social Security has made and is making a tremendous contribution to the strengthening of the social, economic, political and moral life of our nation. Those who seek to weaken the foundation on which it rests are rendering America a great disservice. Those who seek to strengthen the foundation, however, are rendering a service not only to this generation, but to generations yet unborn. (Bender & Leone, 1990, p. 140)

Despite the general success of social security in reducing poverty among the elderly, significant gaps remain. Some observers, such as Gilder (1990), maintain that those in the low income brackets are there only temporarily. Many *are* able to move up the scale, but the fact remains that certain groups constitute a disproportionate share of the poor and face often insurmountable obstacles to breaking the poverty cycle. Even with the War on Poverty's Community Action Program teaching the poor how to organize and compete on a more even footing politically and economically, those in the lowest income groups still lack the education, skills, resources, and leadership to take full advantage of all the options available to them. Consequently the middle class often benefits more from social welfare programs than do the poor.

The key that opens the door to most of our major social welfare programs is employment, and it is steady employment that many of the poor cannot achieve. Of the 11 social welfare programs on which the government spends most heavily, 6 are for people who are working or have worked and 5 are for those who do not work or have not worked. Because many of these people do not or cannot work, the poor tend to benefit less than the middle class from the major contributory social insurance programs and are forced to rely more heavily on the less adequate noncontributory social assistance programs. Under Ronald Reagan these gaps tended to widen as social insurance programs benefiting largely the middle classes were expanded even as the social assistance programs on which the poor are more dependent were cut back. Progress has been made in addressing the needs of the poor, especially among the elderly, but adequacy remains a problem for many. Though retirement for most is no longer a sentence to poverty, many persons are forced to live on less income than they were accustomed to during their years of gainful employment. On the average, social security provides about 40% of preretirement income. Forty-five percent of the elderly still are either poor or economically vulnerable. The poor are much less likely to be protected by private pensions and medical insurance, less likely to qualify for unemployment benefits, and less likely to be able to afford the down payment on a home. Minimal benefits under current social welfare programs do not provide a decent standard of living for most poor people.

Though social security enjoys rather broad popular support and is viewed by many as a necessary component of policy if government is concerned with providing its citizens a decent and just environment in which to live, developments over the last two decades have prompted growing numbers to question whether the system needs some rethinking and redirection. This issue will be pursued further in Chapter 7.

3

Hunger in America

In *The Other America* Michael Harrington (1962) chided his fellow Americans with these words: "I want to tell every well-fed and optimistic American that it is intolerable that so many millions should be maimed in body and in spirit when it is not necessary that they should be" (p. 652). Because hunger and malnutrition are hard to define and often for the large part virtually unseen, they are issues over which there has been and continues to be considerable disagreement, however. Throughout our early history, hunger was a matter addressed by private charities, with governments getting involved only temporarily during severe economic downturns. All of this changed with the Great Society programs of the 1960s and their broad attack on poverty and its various manifestations in U.S. society.

In the mid to late 1960s various welfare, labor, and philanthropic organizations along with several liberal Northern members of Congress began to push hunger as a major social issue to be addressed on the national level. Largely through the efforts of this coalition, hunger emerged as a separate social issue and began to attract widespread attention. In 1967 the Field Foundation set the snowball in motion when it sent a survey team out to check the incidence of hunger and malnutrition among poor Americans. Although suspecting that many among the poor were suffering from hunger and malnourishment, not even the investigators were prepared for what they encountered. Invited to accompany the team on a trip, then-Senator George Murphy (R., CA) observed: "I didn't know that we were going to be dealing with the situation of starving people and starving youngsters" (Physicians Task Force on Hunger, 1988, p. 46). The task force of physicians reported:

> Wherever we went and wherever we looked, we saw children in significant numbers who were hungry and sick, children for whom hunger is a daily fact of life, and sickness in many forms an inevitability. The children we saw were more than just malnourished. They were hungry, weak, apathetic. Their lives are being shortened. They are visibly and predictably losing their health, their energy, their spirits. They are suffering from hunger and disease, and directly or indirectly, they are dying from them— which is exactly what "starvation" means. (Physicians Task Force on Hunger, 1985, p. 46)

"In child after child we saw evidence of vitamin and mineral deficiencies . . . associated with poor food intake," reported the physicians. "Malnutrition" is not what we found; we found "starvation" (p. 46).

Other groups began to press the cause. The Citizens Board of Inquiry into Hunger and Malnutrition reported in April 1968 that in a nationwide study of food programs it found that over 300 of the nation's poorest counties had no food assistance programs in operation. The board estimated that as many as 10-14.5 million Americans were seriously underfed (*Congress and the Nation*, 1965, p. 778). At about the same time the national Committee on School Lunch Participation released its report, which also was highly critical of existing government food and nutrition programs. On May 21, 1968, CBS television aired a documentary entitled "Hunger in America" in which it reported cases of serious malnutrition in the South. The Citizens' Crusade Against Poverty organized its own nationwide study titled "Hunger U.S.A.," and in testimony before the Subcommittee on Employment of the Senate Labor and Public Welfare Committee, the Reverend Ralph Abernathy, leader of the Southern Christian Leadership Conference and head of the Poor People's Campaign, stated: "We cannot let Americans starve because Agriculture Committees choose to dislike the poor. . . . Hunger in America must be abolished, and we cannot compromise on that fact" (*Congress and the Nation,* 1969, p. 778).

Not everyone agreed the problem was as pronounced and widespread as these reports claimed. Secretary of Agriculture Orville Freeman described the CBS documentary as a "biased, one-sided, dishonest presentation of a serious national problem" (*Congress and the Nation,* 1969, p. 778). Congressman W. R. Poage (D., TX), chairman of the House Committee on Agriculture, responded, "The report was quite inaccurate and misleading to put it mildly. There seems to be little or no evidence," he claimed, "that any substantial hunger in this country exists" (p. 592). On June 16, 1968, the House Agriculture Committee countered with its own hunger study, reporting that statements from county officials "lead to the unmistakable conclusion that there is very little actual hunger in the United States, but widespread malnutrition caused largely by ignorance as to what constitutes a balanced diet" (p. 592).

While arguments over the definition and extent of hunger continued, it became clear that large numbers of Americans suffered from malnutrition, inadequate diets, and hunger, and pressures mounted for some response. At the prompting of Senator Robert Kennedy (D., NY) the Senate Labor and Public Welfare Committee established the Subcommittee on Poverty. The Select Committee on Nutrition and Human Needs was created in 1967 with Senator George McGovern (D., SD) as its chairman. In 1969 President Nixon convened the White House Conference on Nutrition, and he observed: "There can be no doubt that hunger and malnutrition exist in America and that some millions may be affected" (Nixon, 1969).

With more and more groups such as the National Council of Churches, the Interfaith Coalition Against Hunger, the Urban Coalition, the National Council on Hunger, the Poor People's Campaign, the League of Women Voters, and the U.S. Conference of Mayors joining the push, Congress passed more than a dozen food aid bills from 1967 to 1980 (see Table 3.1). Spending on food programs grew more than 500%. This drive stimulated some of the largest programs of the Great Society.

In spite of the Field Foundation's follow-up study in 1977, which reported that "America's nutrition programs had succeeded" (p. 47) and the investigators no longer encountered widespread hunger, by the late 1960s and early 1970s a backlash against Great Society programs, including the food programs, had set in. The programs came in for heavy criticism for spending too much, creating welfare dependency, wasting taxpayers' funds, and being corrupt and inefficient. The consensus that had earlier supported these programs disappeared, paving the way for Ronald Reagan and his leadership of a conservative assault on social spending programs, including food aid programs.

The Reagan-initiated cuts in social spending coupled with the extended recession of the early 1980s moved hunger back onto the agenda

Table 3.1 Federal Food Assistance Programs, Legislative Summary

1935	Agriculture Trade Act—Section 32 gave the Secretary of Agriculture discretionary authority to use a portion of customs receipts on imported agricultural products to purchase surplus farm commodities for distribution to poor persons.
1936	School Lunch Program—Started under authority given to the Secretary of Agriculture to reduce farm surpluses.
1946	National School Lunch Act—Gave permanent status to the program started under Secretary of Agriculture authority.
1962	Amendment to School Lunch Act—Authorized special below-cost meals for children from needy families.
1964	Food Stamp Act—Provides food stamps to needy persons for purchase of foodstuffs. Act formalized programs started in the 1930s by President Roosevelt and revived in 1961 by President Kennedy.
1974, 1975	Amended to eliminate initial purchase requirement, which prevented some poorer people from participating, and extend eligibility to more needy persons.
1965	Older Americans Act—Includes meals for the needy elderly.
1966	Child Nutrition Act—Food support to provide more balanced diets for children in needy families.
1972	Women, Infants and Children Act (WIC)—Provides food assistance for poor pregnant or nursing mothers and their infants.
1983	Temporary Emergency Food Assistance Program (TEFAP) —Provided food aid to the homeless.
1987	Homeless Assistance Act—Expanded food programs for the homeless.

See Table 3.2 for numbers of participants and expenditures on Food Programs.

of public debate. By the mid-1980s various groups were pointing to hunger and malnutrition as growing problems. A 1983 study by the Department of Health and Human Services reported that 10% to 15% of infants born to migrant worker and other poor rural families did not grow properly because of dietary deficiencies (Kotz, 1984, p. 20). A 1983 study at Cook County Hospital in Chicago showed a sharp increase in the number of infants admitted over the previous few years with nutrition and growth problems (Kotz, 1984, p. 20). The Citizen's Commission on Hunger in New England reported in February 1984, "We find that a series of clear and conscious policy decisions—some made more than a decade ago, some made within the last three years— have increased hunger in America" (p. 19). Another indication of growing hunger was the rise in the numbers participating in emergency food programs. The Center on Budget and Policy Priorities surveyed 181 emergency food programs and 80% of them reported serving more people in 1983 than in 1982, some as many as 100% more. Programs in 20 major cities reported a 71% increase in their emergency feeding efforts (Kotz, 1984).

In its 1985 follow-up on its earlier studies, the Physicians Task Force on Hunger reported hunger and malnutrition were again serious national problems. Although not as bad as two decades earlier, said the team, "hunger in the U.S. is now more widespread and serious than at any time in the last ten to fifteen years" (p. 48). They found the problem grew significantly in the 1980s and they found no city or state in which there was not extensive hunger. "Hunger," they said, "is a problem of epidemic proportions across the nation" (p. 48).

As a result of the renewed debate in the 1980s regarding the incidence of hunger, the Food Research and Action Center of Washington, D.C., conducted a 3-year door-to-door survey in seven areas of the country to determine the level of hunger that existed. The resulting report constitutes the most comprehensive look to date at childhood hunger, and according to the executive director of the center, Robert Fersh, "paints a disturbing picture of the day-to-day struggle of low-income households to maintain a nutritionally adequate diet" (*Daily News,* 1991, p. 6-A). According to the report, 5.5 million children—one in eight—go hungry and another 6 million are "at risk." Altogether, the Center reported, one-fourth of the nation's youngsters under age 12 suffer from food shortage problems. The study found that many poor families had to spend so much of their income for shelter, what was left was not adequate for food. In 1987 a typical family spent about 22% of its income on shelter; in 1990 many of the poorest families surveyed spent more than 60% of their income on shelter, leaving some only $0.68 per person a month for food. The study found that hungry children from such poor families were absent from school almost twice as much as other youngsters, and the authors warned that if the problems went unattended, the hungry children would be less productive as adults and "our society will be less competitive in the world marketplace." The report concluded a boost in federal funding could solve the problem ("Study details struggle of needy for proper diet," 1991; "Survey finds one in eight children hungry," 1991).

Conservative sources disputed such conclusions. President Reagan's Task Force on Food Assistance reported that although "we cannot doubt that there is hunger in America," there is little systematic evidence of widespread or increasing undernutrition in the United States. Saying "hunger can neither be positively reported nor definitely proved," they recommended "thorough studies" of the problem. George G. Graham (1985), physician, professor at Johns Hopkins University, and a member of the task Force, wrote in the *Public Interest* that the United States had the most abundant and least expensive food supply in the world. How could hunger be a problem, he asked? (p. 3). Anna Kondratas (1988), an employee with the U.S. Department of Agriculture, pointing out that 1 in 10 Americans received food stamps, said the problem of hunger was greatly exaggerated. Hunger, she said, was a "subjective impression" and the current "perception of widespread hunger is rooted in subjective, anecdotal impression, based on isolated and unrepresentative cases." Only isolated cases of hunger remain, she insisted, and the degree of hunger in the United States was "comparatively tiny," with persistent hunger related more to "dietary ignorance than to lack of federal assistance" (p. 51). She contended:

> The problem of hunger in America has been vastly exaggerated in recent years. Although there is no credible methodology for determining the exact extent, the evidence suggests strongly that there is no mass hunger in America and that there has been no major change in the nutritional status of Americans in recent years. (1986, p. 97)

Members of Congress tended to disagree. Representative Leon Panetta (D, CA) observed, "This country faces a very serious problem with regard to hunger," and his colleague Representative Mark Andrews (R, ND) stated, "Although there are several emergency problems of concern . . . hunger is probably the most prevalent and the most insidious." (*Congress and the Nation,* 1985, p. 600.

Major Issues

A part of the reason for the differences among those on either side of this issue is the absence of any clear definitions for hunger and malnutrition and any precise methods or yardsticks for measuring the incidence of each. Those who question these programs claim the numbers who suffer from hunger and undernourishment are much smaller than the 10-20 million claimed by the proponents. Graham (1985) argued, "Despite vehement claims to the contrary, the most careful and objective analysis reveals what common observation would assert: that there is little evidence of major or even significant hunger and malnutrition in this country, unless some whimsical definitions . . . are used for those two terms" (p. 17). The conservative critics also question the methodology used in many of the studies of hunger and malnutrition, claiming that the researchers equate living in poverty with being hungry and malnourished (Graham, 1985; Kondratas, 1986, 1988). This, they maintain, inflates the numbers beyond those who are really hungry. They discount the results of many reports on hunger as being largely anecdotal and methodologically unsound. On the Physicians Task Force's (1985) report, *Hunger in America: The Growing Epidemic,* Kondratas (1986) wrote of the estimate of 20 million hungry Americans, "The statistic bears no relation to fact. The study simply ignored the dietary surveys available to any analyst, which find that the majority of the poor have perfectly adequate diets; and that many non-poor have inadequate ones" (p. 93). Graham went even further: "Future generations could have good reason to accuse this one of dumping these unwanted surplus foods on the poor, contributing to the high incidence among them of obesity, diabetes, and degenerative vascular disease" ("WIC works," 1991, p. A11).

The liberal proponents of food programs point out that hunger and malnourishment often go unrecognized because the symptoms may be easily mistaken. Some hungry people may actually be overweight because their diets rely heavily on starches and fats. Lethargy caused by hunger is often mistaken for laziness and illnesses stemming from hunger and malnourishment may be attributed to other causes. The effects of undiagnosed hunger can be devastating, point out the proponents, especially among children and the elderly. Malnourishment in pregnant mothers can lead to low birth weights, higher than average infant mortality rates, and infants with mental or physical defects. In young children hunger and inadequate diets can retard both mental and physical development. In school, children who are hungry have trouble paying attention and do not learn as well as others. A study by the Boston University School of Medicine and Public Health and the Tufts University School of Nutrition showed that elementary students from low-income families who participated in the school breakfast program showed greater improvement on their standardized test scores and had less tardiness and absence than those from similar backgrounds who did not participate. On a scale of 200 to 800, children who ate breakfast at school improved their scores an average of 48.4 points over the previous year. Those not receiving breakfast improved by only 40.9 points

("Hungry children cannot learn," 1991, p. 4). Supporters of the food programs for children maintain that a hungry child cannot learn effectively. And a child who cannot learn, they point out, becomes an adult who is ill prepared for the workplace and cannot compete economically. Employers are becoming more aware of such problems, as was attested to by the fact that when hearings were held on refunding the WIC program in 1991 among those testifying on behalf of the program were the top executives of five major U.S. corporations. They said the country's labor pool was becoming inferior because of nutritional problems among the poor ("Committee plan would boost WIC spending," 1991). Critics reject most of these arguments as unfounded. They attribute differences in birth weights and growth rates to racial, ethnic, and genetic factors, not nutrition and diet. Graham (1985) called the argument that poor school performance is related to hunger a "simplistic concept" (p. 5).

Some conservatives opposed food aid because of a fear these programs would become welfare programs contributing to the dependency of poorer persons. Nick Kotz, author of several books and articles on hunger, responded: "Those who worry about more food aid encouraging a 'dole mentality' should be reassured that a hungry child cannot learn and an ill-fed adult cannot compete for and hold a job" (1978, p. 22).

The food aid programs are also criticized as being corrupt, wasteful, and inefficient. Conservative critics contend that cheating and fraud are widespread in the food programs and that many people receive benefits who do not need them. They are also critical of a system providing multiple benefits under a variety of programs. They contend that the programs are wasteful and ineffective because many recipients fail to use their benefits wisely and spend their freed-up income on nonessentials.

Admitting some fraud and abuse as inevitable in these types of programs, the liberal proponents point out numerous studies and reports that document the effectiveness of the food programs. The Congressional Budget Office reported that almost all food stamps went to people who needed them, 87% to people with incomes below the poverty level (Kotz, 1978). Catherine A. Bertini, assistant secretary of Agriculture for Food and Consumer Services, said, "There's basic agreement that people who are receiving benefits are those who should" (Kosterlitz, 1990a, p. 389). Over half of the households receiving food stamps have gross incomes of less than $3,600 per year and 93% of the recipients have disposable assets of less than $500 each. Some 78% of recipients are children, elderly, disabled, or single-parent households (Kotz, 1978, p. 21). Besides, point out proponents, food aid is about the only assistance available to poor working people, providing an element of equity and fairness in social welfare spending. The budget office found that food stamp benefits raised about 4 million working poor above the poverty level (Kotz, 1978, p. 21). Donald A. West, an agricultural economist at Washington State University, studied the food spending patterns of families at different income levels. His conclusion was that "food stamp" families were not "wasting" their dollars, but purchased "staples" largely. Studies indicate such families use 57% of their stamp allotment for additional food purchases and 43% to free up their regular income for other basic needs such as rent, fuel, and clothing (Kotz, 1978, p. 21). The money was not being spent frivolously in most cases. In response to the critics' concerns over multiple benefits, defenders point out that at best benefits under these programs are minimal. The food stamp program, for example, is designed to provide only 70% of a family's basic food needs. Even with very prudent shopping, such benefits provide only a minimal diet and many families run out of food before the end of the month. One food stamp recipient described his family's plight in these words: "There is a hell, and I've been there. It's when a man has a family to support, has his health, is ready to work, and there's no work to do. When he stands with empty hands and sees his children going hungry" (Kotz, 1984, p. 23). This man's family existed on rice and ketchup when their food stamps ran out each month. So, even with current efforts, the proponents point out, many Americans still have inadequate diets. About 12% of the population consume less than the recommended daily amount of protein and as high as 30%-40% have other dietary deficiencies.

Findings simply do not support the critics' claims of ineffectiveness, proponents claim. As a result of preschool and school lunch and breakfast programs, the diets of millions of children have been improved. The budget office reported a marked improvement in the nutrition of poor children, supporters point out. Likewise, the WIC program, which provides supplemental food assistance to pregnant women, infants, and young children, has helped improve their health levels. One study estimated that WIC has reduced future health care costs by $3 for each dollar spent ("Aid to poor seen as cost effective," 1985), and a 1990 study by Mathematics Policy Research for the Department of Agriculture found that women receiving WIC packages during pregnancy required medicaid spending as much as $598 less than mothers and children 60 days after birth who received no aid ("WIC works," 1991). Food aid proponents also call attention to the Field Foundation (1977) follow-up study on hunger. In its second report, the team noted, "There was a sharp contrast between the bright-eyed, happy and alert little ones we saw in the Head Start centers and the dull, listless infants and children we saw who did not participate" (Kotz, 1978, p. 22). Food assistance programs do work, maintain the proponents; they simply are not currently reaching enough needy people.

Efforts at Solution

Food Stamps

The first food assistance programs undertaken by the federal government were designed primarily to reduce surpluses and raise farm income; aiding the poor was a secondary objective. In this vein the first food stamp program was started in 1939 in New York City to distribute surplus commodities to persons on relief. Participants could purchase $1 to $1.50 worth of orange food stamps per family member each week and they were given 50 cents worth of blue stamps that could be exchanged for commodities. The commodities distribution program was continued in various forms from that date.

The modern version of the food stamp program was started on a trial basis by President Kennedy in eight test areas in 1961. Three years later it was enacted into law by Congress in the Food Stamp Act of 1964. Signing the bill on August 31, 1964, President Johnson said the measure provided "one of our most valuable weapons for the War on Poverty" and a step toward "the fuller and wiser use of our agricultural abundance" (*Congress and the Nation,* 1965, p. 741). Aimed at aiding low-income families to improve their diet, the food stamp program reflects Americans' ambivalence on social assistance programs. It shows a desire to see that the poor are fed, but at the same time a distrust of their ability to make responsible spending choices. So they are provided coupons redeemable for food products but not for cash.

The food stamp program was to replace the old commodities distribution program, which had a number of problems. It was not directed to dietary balance as it was limited to commodities in which there were surpluses. Recipients had to travel to central depot points for distribution, sometimes a problem for poor persons, especially the elderly. Because commodities were regarded as a government dole, there was a stigma factor. Critics also charged that the program reduced purchases of commercial food. The new food stamp program would provide more variety and nutrition in poor people's food choices, reduce the stigma because they would purchase their food in commercial markets, help farmers by stimulating food purchases by the poor, and help food retailers through increased sales.

At first under the new program counties could choose to substitute food stamps for the older commodities program. But when some counties were slow to switch to the new approach, the 1974 amendments required all counties to adopt food stamps. Also under the original act recipients were required to purchase the stamps, and this requirement kept some of those most in need from participating. A family of four, for example, with an income of $300 per month was required to come up with $83 in cash to get $182 worth of food stamps. For an extremely poor family, making even a minimal cash payment could be most difficult. In the 1974 amendments the purchase requirement was dropped, making the program more accessible to the really needy. The food stamp program is the only social program available to all low-income people; many people ineligible for other forms of welfare are eligible for food stamps.

The food stamp program grew slowly at first, but by 1970 outlays for antihunger programs had doubled over 1965. In 1968 the government spent $288 million on food stamps for 2.8 million recipients; 10 years later the figure was $5 billion for 15 million recipients. The program continued to grow until 1981 when the Reagan administration tightened eligibility requirements and over 1 million recipients were dropped from the rolls. Reagan also targeted the program for spending cuts and the General Accounting Office estimated that the program got $7 billion less in 1982 to 1985 than it would have received without the Reagan cuts (Kosterlitz, 1990a, p. 389). The number of recipients fluctuates, increasing during times of economic recession and higher unemployment. In 1985, reacting to reports of increasing hunger, Congress expanded both benefits and eligibility under the food stamp program. With the number of participants approaching 20 million, Congress approved a $523 million increase over 5 years, authorizing $13.03 billion for FY 1986, increasing to $15.97 billion by FY 1990. Under the new guidelines AFDC and SSI recipients were automatically eligible for food stamps.

School Lunch Program

The federal school lunch program was started in 1936 under special authority granted to the Secretary of Agriculture (a major objective of the program was to reduce surpluses of certain farm commodities). The program was given permanent status in the National School Lunch Act of 1946. A 1962 amendment authorized special below-cost meals for children from needy families. This program, like the food stamp program, grew substantially in the 1960s and 1970s. In 1968 the program provided 3 million lunches and 300,000 breakfasts for children from low-income backgrounds. By 1978 the program was providing 10.6 million free lunches, 1.3 million subsidized lunches, and 2.6 million free breakfasts.

Other Food Programs

One of the oldest programs of food assistance was created under Section 32 of the 1935 Agriculture Trade Act, which allows the Secretary of Agriculture to use a portion of customs receipts on imported agriculture products to purchase surplus commodities and distribute them to needy persons. Agriculture secretaries have been criticized by food program advocates for not exercising this discretionary authority more extensively.

In 1966 Congress passed the Child Nutrition Act and various programs aimed at improving nutrition provide meals for preschool youngsters from low-income families. The WIC program provides food assistance for pregnant mothers, infants, and children. It has grown from only $14 million appropriated in 1974 to $1.58 billion in 1986, $1.78 billion in 1989, and $2.35 billion for 1990-1991. The program has been attributed with helping to reduce birth defects and mental retardation resulting from malnutrition of women and fetuses. The program still reaches less than one third of those eligible for assistance. WIC was one of only a couple of social programs targeted by President Bush for increases in his proposed FY 1992 budget.

Other related programs include those providing meals for the elderly, the Summer Food Service Program, and the Nutrition Education and Training Program, aimed at helping low-income people learn about nutrition and how they can develop better food shopping and dietary habits. (See Table 3.2 and Figure 3.1 for past and projected federal expenditures on food assistance programs.)

Conclusion

Since the 1960s food assistance programs have grown by over 600% and the food stamp program now helps more Americans than any social

Table 3.2 Participants and Expenditures for Food Programs, 1970-1988

Program	Unit	1970	1980	1981	1982	1983	1984	1985	1986	1987	1988
Food Stamp:											
Participants	Million	4.3	21.1	22.4	21.7	21.6	20.9	19.9	19.4	19.1	18.6
Federal cost	Mil. dol	550	8,721	10,630	10,208	11,152	10,696	10,744	10,605	10,500	11,149
Nutrition Assistance Program for Puerto Rico:											
Federal cost	Mil. dol	(x)	(x)	(x)	206	825	825	825	820	853	879
National School Lunch Program (NSLP):											
Free lunches served	Million	739	1,671	1,737	1,622	1,714	1,702	1,657	1,678	1,656	1,652
Reduced-price lunches served	Million	(NA)	308	312	262	253	248	255	257	259	262
Children participating	Million	22.4	26.6	25.8	22.9	23.0	23.4	23.6	23.7	23.9	24.2
Federal cost	Mil. dol	300	2,279	2,381	2,185	2,402	2,508	2,578	2,714	2,797	2,908
School Breakfast (SB):											
Children participating	Million	.5	3.6	3.8	3.3	3.4	3.4	3.4	3.5	3.6	3.7
Federal cost	Mil. dol	11	288	332	317	344	364	379	406	447	474
Special School Milk:											
Quantity reimbursed	Mil. 1/2 pt.	2,902	1,795	1,533	202	189	174	167	162	163	194
Federal cost	Mil. dol	101	145	101	18	17	16	16	15	15	19
Women-Infant-Children:											
Participants	Million	(x)	2.0	2.2	2.3	2.7	3.2	3.3	3.5	3.6	3.8
Federal cost	Mil. dol	(x)	603	729	785	937	1,156	1,235	1,304	1,379	1,484
Child Care Feeding (CC):											
Children participating	Million	.1	.7	.8	.8	.9	1.0	1.0	1.1	1.2	1.3
Federal cost	Mil. dol	6	207	303	290	305	348	390	427	476	537

continued

53

Table 3.2 Continued

Program	Unit	1970	1980	1981	1982	1983	1984	1985	1986	1987	1988
Summer Feeding (SF):											
Children participating	Million	.2	1.9	1.9	1.4	1.4	1.4	1.5	1.5	1.6	1.6
Federal cost	Mil. dol	2	106	101	81	95	94	101	106	114	118
Needy Family Commodity:											
Participants	Million	3.8	.1	.1	.1	.1	.1	.1	.1	.1	.1
Federal cost	Mil. dol	282	24	29	33	35	40	47	49	49	47
Nutrition Program for the Elderly:											
Meals served	Million	(x)	166	185	189	201	213	225	228	232	241
Federal cost	Mil. dol	(x)	75	94	101	120	127	134	137	139	145

SOURCE: U.S. Dept. of Agriculture, Food and Nutrition Service. In *Agricultural Statistics*, annual; and unpublished data (Reprinted in U.S. Bureau of the Census, 1990, p. 365).

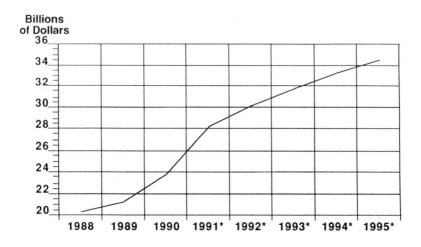

Figure 3.1. Federal Expenditures on Food Assistance Programs, 1988-1995
*Estimated
SOURCE: Budget of the United States, 1991.

program besides social security. Nevertheless, in a nation with the most abundant food supplies in the world, there are still millions of persons existing on inadequate diets. In spite of all the steps taken thus far, there are still gaps in the system. At the start of the 1990s less than 75% of the eligible poor were receiving food stamps (Kosterlitz, 1990a, p. 389), and Johanna Dwyer of Tufts University's School of Nutrition estimated that hundreds of thousands of elderly persons were malnourished and sick because they were not eating proper diets (Duston, 1991). Many feel the Thrifty Food Plan to which food stamp allocations are tied is too meager and is based on several assumptions that are unrealistic in the economy of the 1990s. For example, the maximum value for a car owned by a recipient is $4,500. This figure was set in 1977 and since then the Consumer Price Index for used car values has jumped by 120%. Poor families' rent costs have soared and almost one half of poor renters pay 60%-70% of their income for rent. They are allowed to deduct only $177 per month from their income in determining food stamp eligibility; thus some of the poorest get less in food stamps because of what they now have to pay for rent. Likewise, improved collection of child support payments may reduce a family's eligibility for food stamps.

Congress did approve a 3% adjustment in the Thrifty Food Plan to start with FY 1991, but the adjustment is based on prices in June of the previous year, meaning adjustments remain 3 to 15 months behind (see Kosterlitz, 1990a, p. 391).

Food programs are under the purview of the Agriculture committees in Congress and the U.S. Department of Agriculture; both tend to be rather conservative in their approach to the hunger issue. And although food assistance programs have rather solid bipartisan congressional support as well as the support of the food industry, over the last decade our leaders allowed hunger to worsen. An adequate system for monitoring and measuring the incidence of hunger is still lacking, and millions of those who are eligible still are not participating. The Department of Agriculture needs to press state and local governments to engage in better informational programs that will make potential recipients more aware of the benefits available. Building on its past successes, the government needs to expand the food stamp, school lunch, WIC, and related programs to meet the food and nutritional needs of all low-income persons. Simply relying on overall economic growth and advancement is not an adequate policy for meeting the needs of those who are hungry.

4

Homeless in America

Until recently most Americans tended to associate shantytowns, makeshift shelters, and overcrowded, deteriorating dwellings with underdeveloped areas of the world. But growing media attention and numerous studies in the 1980s revealed that for increasing numbers of Americans in or near poverty, adequate housing was a growing problem.

What focused national attention on this issue was the growing number of homeless in our society. Although there was little agreement as to their numbers—the federal Department of Housing and Urban Development (HUD) estimated 300,000, whereas advocacy groups claimed as many as 3 million—the problem certainly gained much more visibility among the general public and consequently in Congress. As a result of the efforts of such advocates as the late Mitch Snyder and media figures like Martin Sheen and Valerie Harper, the image of the homeless changed. Once perceived as primarily bums and hoboes who did not want to work, the homeless are now seen as being more deserving of public concern and support. Another factor contributing to the changed perception is the different composition of the more recent homeless population. No longer are those who are homeless primarily deinstitutionalized mental patients, drug addicts, alcoholics, and those who simply choose not to work: a U.S. Conference of Mayors' study found that women, children, and entire families were increasingly showing up among the homeless (Kosterlitz, 1987b; Steinbach & Peirce, 1987).

Some reports indicated that as many as one half of the homeless may be families and workers who are without jobs. Women and children are presently the fastest growing group among the homeless (Steinbach, 1989; Steinbach & Peirce, 1987).

Although the homeless themselves, like others caught in the poverty cycle, are often short on coping skills and political influence, their changing profile and increased media attention helped to attract a steadily widening circle of advocates and public support. Many groups normally viewed as nonpolitical joined the movement for more federal assistance. Because it was estimated that at least one third of the homeless were veterans, the American Legion took up the cause. The 1990 annual meeting of the American Psychological Association included 19 hours of discussion on homelessness among its programs. Feeling the increasing burden for services, charity organizations, which form a natural grass-roots lobby on the issue, called for more help from the federal level. Leading the push for more federal involvement are such groups as the National Coalition for the Homeless, which helped to provide greater focus for the issue and draw support groups together behind the cause, the National Low Income Housing Coalition, the Children's Defense Fund, and the National Rural Housing Coalition, among others. Since for the most part the homeless themselves are neither voters nor political activists, such broad-based group support is essential to obtain any political response.

The problem and its growth are issues that cannot be easily ignored. One mother who had been homeless for 13 months told an interviewer, "Homelessness will make you want to die. This country has got to get out of its denial of the problem" (*Courier-Journal,* August 16, 1990, p. A11). A 1987 survey conducted in 25 major cities by the National Coalition for the Homeless showed the number of homeless had grown by 25% and an increasing portion of that number were members of a family in which a parent was working but simply could not find affordable housing in areas where the turnover rate in available housing was frequently as low as 1% annually. In New York City the number of persons staying in public shelters for the homeless grew from 2,000 in 1978 to over 10,000 in 1987 (Rauch, 1988; Steinbach, 1989; Steinbach, 1990; Steinbach & Peirce, 1987). Such conditions prompted growing concerns on a number of fronts. Barry Zigas, director of the National Low Income Housing Coalition, called conditions "the worst since the Great Depression" (Steinbach & Peirce, 1987, p. 1465), and Leon Weiner, past president of the National Association of Home Builders, cautioned, "Homelessness is not the tip of the iceberg because icebergs are cool. It is the core of a volcano" (Steinbach, 1989, p. 851). The mounting problem has not gone unnoticed in Congress, where Senator Pete V. Domenici (R., NM) warned, "We've been hiding our heads in the sand under the guise of fiscal responsibility" (Kosterlitz, 1987b, p. 493).

The homeless persons crowding the available shelters and sleeping in public buildings and on sidewalk grates and park benches are the most visible signs of a housing shortage, but they are only a part of the total problem. Thousands more are living in overcrowded, deteriorating, vermin- and crime-infested, substandard dwellings unfit for human habitation. William C. Apgar, Jr., director of the Joint Center for Housing Studies at Harvard, noted, "The state of the nation's housing is not good. There is no single housing problem, but a series of interconnected problems" (Steinbach, 1989, p. 851).

Like so many areas in our affluent and highly productive U.S. society, housing poses a paradox. Though a majority of Americans are better housed than at any previous point in our history and live in safe, stable neighborhoods, growing numbers of their fellow citizens are without homes or live in housing that fails to meet minimal standards of decency.

The availability of suitable housing at prices people can afford is becoming more and more a problem. As the gap between incomes and the cost of housing continues to widen, growing numbers of people are frustrated in their efforts to attain acceptable housing. Barry Zigas of the National Low Income Housing Coalition observed, "People are desperate, they're mad and they're frustrated" (Steinbach, 1989, p. 851). At the start of the 1990s, the nation faces a housing "shortfall" of 2-3 million units per year (Rauch, 1988; Steinbach, 1989; Steinbach, 1990; Steinbach & Peirce, 1987). With the high demand driving prices up, most low-income and even lower-middle-income persons have been squeezed out of the market already. A National League of Cities survey of 444 cities around the nation indicated problems of "severe proportions" in most when it came to finding housing for homeless and low-income renters (Steinbach & Peirce, 1987, p. 1465).

In 1980 the government set as a national benchmark on expenditures for housing, 30% of family income; amounts beyond that figure were to be considered excessive. Since 1981 rental costs have risen 16% faster than the consumer price index while the median income for renters dropped about $2,500. As three of five low-income families are renters, they are caught in a cost crunch. A 1985 Census Bureau survey reported over 22 million families paying more than the 30% housing cost threshold and another 9 million living in substandard or over-crowded facilities. In 1985, 45% of all households below the official poverty level paid at least 70% of their total income on rent and utilities. Sixty-three percent of low-income renters spent at least half their income on housing and 85% of them paid 30% or more on rent and utilities. The Joint Center for Housing Studies of Harvard and MIT found that in 1986 about one third of all single mothers spent approximately 75% of their income for rent and that 5 million households with income under $5,000 per year averaged two thirds of their income spent on rent. At the same time, the center found that many rental apartments around the country were unoccupied because low-income persons could not afford the rent, which ranged from $400 to $900 per month (Steinbach, 1990a, pp. 570-571). A 1985 Census Bureau survey reported 11.5 million units of housing vacant. But in many instances either the rents are too high or the units are substandard. As a result of the rising costs, eviction rates among renters are increasing, and more and more persons either become homeless or are forced to move in with parents or relatives. Michael E. Stone of the Economic Policy Institute found in a 1990 study that 78 million Americans were "shelter poor," meaning they spent so much of their income for housing they were unable to afford other basic necessities (p. 2159).

Adding to the problem is a continuing decline in the supply of low-income housing (see Tables 4.1, 4.2, and 4.3). From 1976 through 1982 the federal government subsidized the construction of about 1 million new units of housing for the poor. The tax changes of the Reagan years reduced the subsidies for builders, and since 1986 fewer than 25,000 new units per year are being built. At the same time, many units of less expensive housing are being lost. Since the 1970s about 2 million lower-cost apartments have been demolished as a part of urban renewal or other projects. These usually have not been replaced. Many lower-cost units are in privately owned buildings subsidized by the federal government, and once the mortgages are paid off and contracts restricting rents expire, the owners can use the facilities for whatever purposes they desire. According to a General Accounting Office survey, many owners indicated they would probably take their property off the low-income housing market (Steinbach, 1989). Consequently, GAO has projected the potential loss of as many as 900,000 units by the year 2000. This trend, coupled with curtailed federal subsidies virtually ending private builders' efforts in producing new units, means growing shortages of low-cost housing during the 1990s. And at the same time

Table 4.1 Low-Income Public Housing Units Occupied and Under Construction, 1960-1990

Year	Total (thousands)	Units Occupied	Units Under Construction
1960	593.3	478.2	36.4
1970	1155.3	893.5	126.8
1980	1321.1	1195.6	20.9
1985	1378.0	1344.6	9.6
1986	1365.1	1333.8	12.1
1987	1443.0	1406.4	9.7
1988	1448.8	1413.3	9.7

SOURCE: U.S. Bureau of the Census (1990, p. 726).

availability is shrinking, the number of persons needing housing will grow by about 5 million. Some predictions indicate as many as 18 million homeless Americans over the next 15-20 years. Phillip Clay, housing analyst at MIT, estimated in 1987 that if patterns existing then continued, 17.2 million low-income households would be seeking inexpensive rental housing by the year 2003, but only 9.4 million low-income units would be in existence (Steinbach, 1990a; see also National Housing Preservation Task Force, 1988; Steinbach & Peirce, 1987).

The picture for home ownership has not been bright during the 1980s either (see Figure 4.1). In 1940, 43.6% of American families owned their homes, and by 1980 this figure reached an all-time high of 65.6% then declined to 64% at the start of the 1990s (Wilson, 1990a, p. 1857). Since 1981 home ownership rates have declined steadily as housing costs have soared and mortgage rates remained high. In 1988 the

Table 4.2 Demand for and Availability of Apartments Renting for $250 per Month or Less

Year	Units (millions)	Renters (millions)
1970	9.7	7.3
1978	8.4	8.0
1985	7.9	11.6

SOURCE: U.S. Bureau of the Census (1990).

Table 4.3 Rental Units and Rental Costs, 1980-1988

Year and Rent	Number (thousands)					Percent Rented in 3 Months				
	Total	Northeast	Midwest	South	West	Total	Northeast	Midwest	South	West
1980	196.1	14.2	43.8	91.5	46.6	75	77	77	74	75
1981	135.3	4.9	36.9	68.4	25.1	80	85	86	78	75
1982	117.0	4.6	21.9	66.8	23.7	72	74	79	70	72
1983	191.5	3.5	41.1	115.1	31.8	69	73	86	63	69
1984	313.2	3.8	41.2	194.4	73.9	67	64	79	63	70
1985	365.2	8.1	54.0	166.1	137.0	65	69	72	59	68
1986	407.5	16.9	64.5	171.7	154.5	66	70	70	62	67
1987	345.6	11.3	66.0	124.5	143.9	63	73	65	59	64
1988	284.5	8.5	60.5	92.5	123.0	66	54	73	58	70
Less than $350	17.0	.6	6.9	6.7	2.8	83	79	92	74	84
$350-$449	49.9	.5	13.0	21.4	15.1	71	4	84	61	76
$450-$549	67.6	(z)	15.1	29.7	22.3	66	(z)	71	56	77
$550 or more	150.0	6.9	25.5	34.6	82.9	63	55	64	56	66

z = Less than 500 units.
SOURCE: U.S. Bureau of the Census, *Current Housing Reports*, series H-130 and H-131, and unpublished data.

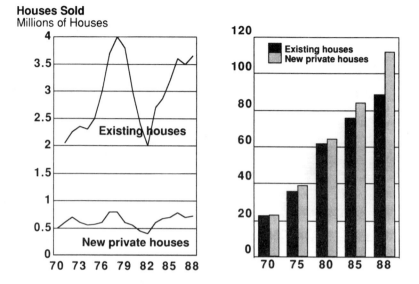

Figure 4.1. Single-Family Houses Sold and Sales Price, 1970-1988
SOURCE: U.S. Bureau of the Census (1990), tables 1263, 1264, and 1266.

National Journal reported that the purchase of a median-priced home would have been accompanied by the following carrying costs as a portion of income: 1949, 14%; 1959, 16%; 1973, 21%; and in 1983, 44% (April 16, 1988, p. 1039). The average price for a home bought in 1988 was $121,910 (for first-time buyers $97,100) and the average monthly mortgage payment was $1,008 or about 32.8% of the buyers' income. Down payments averaged about 15%, up from about 11% in 1985 (Wilson, 1990a, p. 1857). In 1990 the National Association of Home Builders estimated that the purchase of a median-priced home could require a down payment of $11,250 and an annual income of $46,000. These figures have placed the American dream of owning one's home in jeopardy for many, especially for younger families. The sharpest decline in home ownership since 1980 has been among those 35 years of age or younger. For those aged 25-29 the rate declined from 44% to 36% from 1980 to 1988, and for those aged 30-34 the rate went from 61% to 53% (Steinbach, 1989, p. 851). This decline in home ownership exacerbates the home rental problem as well by increasing the demand and driving rent prices even higher.

Even for those who own their home, especially the poor and elderly, everything is not wine and roses. About 40% of the poor own their homes, but for most it is a costly proposition. They paid 47% of their total income, one half of them 50% or more, for their homes, whereas the overall average nationally was only 21%. Although 65% of older Americans own their homes—and many of these houses are paid for—20% of them live in housing not really appropriate for their current conditions. As 70% live in urban areas, 25% in central cities, many live under highly stressful conditions (see Dobelstein, 1990). Large numbers live in older, declining neighborhoods and some are virtually prisoners in their own homes, afraid to take a walk or even go to the market. These are problems extremely difficult to address.

Public Housing

Public housing has not only fallen far short of meeting the needs but also become less and less popular as a viable response to the nation's housing woes. Currently there are 1.4 million units of public housing available, a supply far short of needs in most areas of the country. Local housing authorities in the larger cities report lengthy waiting lists, and no units are available for hundreds of thousands of low-income families who qualify for assistance. Officials in Washington, D.C., report 13,000 on the waiting list; Philadelphia, 23,000; Chicago, 44,000; Miami, 60,000; and New York City, 200,000. Nationwide the waiting lists have reached almost 1 million, and over two thirds of the major cities have closed their rolls to new applicants (Steinbach & Peirce, 1987, p. 1465). Stephen M. Goldfinger of the Massachusetts Mental Health Center stated that Boston could "easily triple the housing available" and still not meet client needs (Kosterlitz, 1990c, p. 2123). Short supply is not the only problem with public housing. Public housing units, owned and managed by 3,000 local public housing authorities under HUD supervision, house the poorest of the nation's poor. The median income for residents is about $6,000 and many projects are poorly managed and maintained. Overcrowded and run down, many public housing projects are in social chaos, havens for drugs, youth gangs, crime, and violence. Due to shortages of maintenance funds, thousands of units are empty and others in a state of advanced decay. As a consequence about 70,000 units annually have to be boarded up and abandoned and about 3,000 per year are demolished. One notorious example of public housing's failure that still sticks in many people's minds is the Pruitt-Igoe project in St. Louis. A huge complex of 12-story high rises, the project was plagued with problems from the outset and the city housing authorities ended up dynamiting and demolishing three blocks—33 buildings, some of which had never been fully occupied. It is issues such as these that lead to a continuing public debate over the proper response of government to our society's housing needs.

Major Issues

Most of the debate over housing policy has centered on meeting the needs of low- and lower-middle-income families. Because the politics of low-income housing is not all that attractive, housing targeted primarily for the poor or near poor has been a persistent issue, but not one high up on the political agenda. To provide adequate housing for the poor the government must either build public housing, subsidize private builders, pay family housing costs, or subsidize private housing owners so the poor can afford the rent.

Major disagreements arise over the scope and methods of government intervention in the provision of housing. Is it more appropriate and effective for the government to finance the construction of new housing or to subsidize rent costs? If subsidies are used, should they go to renters and buyers or to builders and owners?

Many conservatives are philosophically opposed to the government constructing housing, a task which they feel is best left to the private sector. They tend to favor policy that stresses government subsidies and market stimuli to foster growth and competition in the housing market. Liberal supporters of more direct government intervention contend that the market approach produces inadequate supplies, especially of low-cost housing, which is needed most. They say that most builders left on their own will build only more expensive housing because their margin of profit is much greater than on low- and moderate-priced homes. The argument appears correct, as virtually all residential construction since the 1986 changes in the tax laws has been in the luxury class (Steinbach, 1990a, p. 571). The liberals maintain that without federal financing of construction, the private sector will not or cannot provide housing that rents or sells cheaply enough to meet the needs of the poor and near poor. They are skeptical about the adequacy of the trickle-down theory of housing to meet the growing needs of lower-income Americans.

One of the approaches favored most by those opposed to federal construction is a system of rent vouchers or rent subsidies. The conservatives supporting this approach contend that the primary problem is not availability but affordability; Samuel R. Pierce, Jr., Secretary of Housing and Urban Development under President Reagan, said, "The primary housing problem of low-income families nationwide is affordability, not availability, of decent housing" (*Congress and the Nation*, 1989, p. 667). In keeping with this philosophy, Reagan sought during his first term to bring an end to federal subsidies for housing construction, and during his second term he pushed for the widespread use of vouchers in the private housing market. This approach is fine, the liberals say, as long as the supply of low-rent housing is sufficient. It fails, they maintain, when affordable units are not available in sufficient numbers, as often is the case in many cities undergoing economic change and revival in the 1980s and 1990s. The liberals point out that during Reagan's presidency, about one fourth of the available vouchers went unused each year while two thirds of the families eligible for assistance received none (Steinbach, 1990a, p. 571).

Critics of the public housing approach charge that it denies people flexibility and freedom of choice as to where they live and keeps them from having a sense of ownership or pride in their surroundings. Therefore some, including President Bush and current HUD Secretary Jack Kemp, push for the "privatization" of public housing by selling the units to their occupants. The residents then will be in charge of managing their units, and according to the proponents of the approach, will assume greater responsibility for seeing that units are maintained properly and made better places in which to live. In 1989 President Bush sent Congress his Home Ownership and Opportunity for People Everywhere (HOPE) plan. His proposal called for spending increases of $6.8 billion over 3 years, primarily to promote home ownership among low-income renters and public housing tenants. Bush's proposed budgets for FY 1991 and FY 1992 also provided approximately $6.2 billion in Community Development Block Grants for the states, but most of this money came from eliminating all federal funds for constructing public housing. A major feature of the proposal is the provision of $865 million over 2 years to help tenants buy their public housing units. Bush and Kemp hope to sell 8,100 public housing units to tenants by the end of 1992. In briefing members of Congress, Kemp said of the plan: "I think [tenant ownership] . . . is going to save babies, save children, save families and save America" (Guskind & Steinbach, 1991, p. 789). Not everyone, however, shared his optimism for the plan. Congressman William Clay (D., MO) said selling public housing "is a scam the government is trying to perpetrate on the public and rip off the people living in public housing" (p. 799). Mary Ann Russ, executive director of the Council of Large Public Housing Authorities, noted that resident ownership "is very irrelevant to the lives of most public housing tenants. Most of them are really very poor, and they can't afford home ownership even if you give them the units they're living in" (p. 800). Skeptics point out that the average income for families living in public housing in 1991 is about $6,500 per year and about one third of the residents are elderly and on fixed incomes. For many residents affordability is still a major obstacle and many are not likely buyers, claim the critics (p. 803). Expressing doubt about the viability of this approach, Hilbert Fefferman, a private housing consultant, said: "People in public housing are least able to manage home ownership. The notion you can empower the poor requires exceptional leadership and should be encouraged. But you can't give away public housing without a pile of help" (Steinbach, 1989, p. 851).

Addressing the Housing Problem

The primary thrust of federal housing legislation has been to ensure that private housing markets perform in a fashion that will provide adequate housing for citizens at all income levels. The first federal housing legislation was passed by Congress in 1933 and was aimed at protecting housing lenders from financial losses during the Great Depression. This was followed by the Housing Act of 1937, which provided a variety of subsidies to encourage the expansion of the private housing market. During World War II new housing starts dropped to virtually zero, and the end of the war and the return of the soldiers produced a severe housing shortage. Congress quickly established a loan program through the Veterans Administration to help the returning service personnel purchase homes. Following this precedent, Congress over the next several years created the Farmers' Home Administration, the Federal Home Loan Mortgage Association, the Government National Mortgage Association (Ginnie Mae), and the Federal National Mortgage Association (Freddie Mac) to increase the availability of low-cost housing funds by guaranteeing low-interest loans and purchasing mortgages to free up more funds in the private market for housing loans.

These federal initiatives brought improvements in the national housing situation. Between 1940 and 1970 the proportion of U.S. families living in overcrowded housing was reduced from 20% to 9%. In 1940 about 40% of the population lived in substandard dwellings; by 1985 this figure was below 5%. Home ownership grew from 44% in 1940 to a high of almost 64% in 1980 (see Chisman & Pifer, 1987; Wilson, 1990a).

Despite advances in some areas, federal housing policies were proving less productive in other areas. In 1949 urban renewal was launched, with low-cost public housing as its hallmark. The objective was to clean up and revive slum areas by eliminating the deteriorating housing and replacing it with new low-cost public housing. The Housing Act of 1954 expanded urban renewal to include commercial redevelopment as well. Despite congressional encouragement, between 1949 and 1960 only about 250,000 units of public housing were completed, less than 25% of what Congress had authorized. By 1980 the number of public housing units still had reached only 1.3 million, less than 2% of all occupied housing (Dobelstein, 1990). On the whole, urban renewal missed the mark in addressing the housing needs of low-income citizens. In too many instances urban renewal became black removal, eliminating housing in low-income black neighborhoods, then failing to replace it. Also much of the urban renewal funding was used for purposes other than public housing. Furthermore, because some public housing projects turned into slums themselves this approach acquired a bad image.

In the 1957 Housing Act Amendments another element was added to federal housing efforts. This act provided federal support for the costs of rehabilitating declining private housing. Unfortunately this effort came too late, as most of the housing in targeted areas was already beyond rehabilitation. Consequently this attempt to save existing housing was largely a failure.

All in all these federal efforts produced only very limited progress toward the goal of adequate housing for low-income citizens. Consequently, a lack of adequate housing for blacks was a contributing factor to the widespread urban unrest and race riots of the 1960s (Dobelstein,

1990). President Johnson and Congress responded by creating the cabinet-level Department of Housing and Urban Development (HUD) in 1965. Among other tasks, HUD was given the mission of assuring decent housing for all Americans. For the first several years following HUD's establishment housing starts averaged about 1.75 million per year, but fell off to 1.11 million by 1982, far short of meeting the growing needs (Dobelstein, 1990). One of the reasons for this was that even though Congress continued to initiate new programs and appropriate more funds, many of these efforts did very little to increase the supply of adequate housing. The 1968 Housing Act Amendments, for example, launched the Model Cities program to stimulate economic redevelopment in declining urban areas. Under this program the focus shifted from residential to commercial development, and it contributed virtually nothing toward stemming the growing housing shortage. Legislation in 1974 created the Community Development Block Grant program, in which Section 8, Existing Housing and Moderate Rehabilitation, included rent subsidies. This section provided rent vouchers to persons to cover the difference between 30% of their income and the HUD-determined fair market rent they paid for approved housing. Money was shifted from construction subsidies to pay for this program; therefore, if it did anything relative to housing supply, it probably curtailed its expansion.

Although the urban redevelopment and rent subsidy programs helped some low-income families to improve their lives by moving into better neighborhoods, attending better schools, and securing better jobs, these programs did not add greatly to existing housing supplies. In 1973 President Nixon ordered a complete review of federal housing policies. He also imposed a moratorium on new housing construction and impounded housing funds that had already been authorized. For the remainder of his administration primary emphasis was shifted from the construction of new housing to rent subsidies.

Interestingly, President Jimmy Carter, since leaving the White House, has become quite active in Habitat for Humanity, a group engaged in building and renovating housing for poor people. During Carter's administration no new housing legislation was adopted. Carter's successor, Ronald Reagan, came to the White House intent on reducing the federal role in housing. Gerald R. McMurray, staff director for the House Banking Subcommittee on Housing and Community Development, described the Reagan administration approach in these words:

> The Reagan Administration came in with the philosophy that said the federal government had no business doing housing. His people proceeded with great skill to dismantle and terminate programs. Where they couldn't do that, they used the budget process and the bureaucracy to bring programs to a halt. (Steinbach, 1989, p. 853)

Reflecting this attitude, Reagan proposed to eliminate the construction of housing owned and operated by local public housing authorities, rental housing for the elderly and handicapped, rental housing development grants, rental rehabilitation grants, rehabilitation loans and guarantees, and various rural housing programs. Congress refused to go along with all Reagan's proposed cuts, but public housing funds were cut and construction subsidies for building low-income housing were virtually eliminated. During Reagan's first 5 years in office, subsidies for low-income housing were cut by about 60%. Spending on subsidized housing peaked in 1981 at $30.1 billion and by 1989 it had been pared to $7.5 billion. Had Reagan had his way, cuts would have been even deeper, but Congress refused to go along. Emphasis during Reagan's administration was on rent subsidies, a cornerstone of federal housing policy since the Nixon years. Although the numbers receiving such subsidies increased, critics contend this approach does not work when the supply of low-income housing remains severely limited. At the start of Bush's administration, the federal government provided housing subsidies for about 5 million poor through a variety of programs costing about $15 billion per year. Yet, critics point out, a Congressional Budget Office study showed that two thirds of poor households that were eligible for assistance received none (Steinbach, 1990a, p. 571). And, they argue, this approach fails to address the provision of an adequate supply of suitable housing. Critics blame the Reagan administration's cuts for contributing to a multitude of housing woes; among these are growing numbers of homeless, rapid deterioration of existing public housing, increasing shortages of reasonably priced rental housing, and declining rates of home ownership.

Starting in the 1980s much of the attention directed toward housing policy turned to the homeless. Although Americans traditionally tend to blame the poor for their own plight, they blame homelessness on society and are therefore more likely to view this as a problem for the government to address. President Reagan, however, viewed homelessness as primarily a problem for private charity and state and local governments. As media attention grew and public support mounted,

Congress could no longer ignore the plight of the homeless. In 1983 Congress appropriated $100 million to the Federal Emergency Management Administration (FEMA) for an emergency food and shelter program to aid the homeless. This was followed in 1987 with the Homeless Assistance Act, providing for emergency shelters, food, transitional housing, health care, drug and alcohol abuse programs,* job training, and the refurbishing of single-room-occupancy hotels as shelters for the homeless. Though less than enthusiastic about the program, Reagan finally proposed $88 million for it in his 1988 budget and Congress upped the appropriation to $378 million for 1989. President Bush asked for $676 million in his FY 1990 budget. Although funding for the program has grown significantly, it has had its problems. The legislation created the Interagency Council on the Homeless to coordinate the various governmental programs aimed at aiding the homeless, but these programs are spread through six different federal agencies and effective coordination has thus far been a major problem. Some state and local efforts have been more successful and might be looked to as models. St. Louis has developed a Homeless Service Network that is a coalition of various social service agencies. Even though many of these agencies and groups had never worked together before, they have been quite successful in coordinating their efforts to provide a wide range of services to the homeless in their community. The network seeks out available low-rent housing, seeks needed treatment, and provides training in life skills as well as emergency shelter and transition services. Coordinated efforts enable a more comprehensive response to the needs of the homeless than would otherwise be possible.

Two of the most recent initiatives that hold some promise for providing more low-income housing are spin-offs of other legislative policies. Although eliminating most of the previous subsidies for low-income housing, the Tax Reform Act of 1986 added a new provision that is attracting growing interest. The product of a late-night bargain struck by the framers of the 1986 act, this tax credit is targeted strictly toward the provision of rental housing for the truly needy. The credit provides investors a write-off against federal income taxes based on their costs of acquiring, rehabilitating, or constructing housing for low-income persons. The aim of the program is to encourage private sector participation in creating affordable housing. Nonprofit groups across the

---

*Studies indicated that mental illness was a severe problem for 15% to 30% and substance abuse for 30% to 40% of the homeless.

country have used these tax write-offs to attract corporate investors to the support of housing efforts. In 3 years the program produced about 250,000 units of low-income housing. In 1989 about 40 joint public/private projects were undertaken. In 1987 only 18% of the available credits were used, by 1988 68% were used, and in 1990 about 90% were used (Peirce, 1989a, p. 2101). Across the country groups such as the Local Initiatives Support Corporation Enterprise Foundation and the National Community Development Initiative Effort have been founded to bring together local community development corporations (CDCs) and private investors. Through the CDCs and these broker-support groups, investors are encouraged to put money into urban renewal and home-building projects that will provide low-rent shelter for the poor. By 1991 partnerships including CDCs in 20 cities; the Rockefeller Foundation; the Eli Lilly Foundation; Prudential Insurance; and the Hewlett, Knight, and Pew trust funds had been organized. Paul Grogan, president of the Local Initiatives Support Corporation, called the effort "a high-water mark of creative philanthropy in the United States," and John Mutz, the Lilly Foundation president, observed, "It is also elegant in its distribution of risk over a consortium of partners who, together, can address a need of national proportion" (Peirce, 1991a, p. A8). Neal R. Peirce (1991a), a nationally known writer on housing issues, described these efforts as the largest non-government commitment to rebuild poor urban neighborhoods in history: "In a time of federal non-feasance, of near paralysis in housing for poorer Americans, here's a formula emblematic of the novel alliances and approaches the times demand" (p. A8).

The program was assigned to the Treasury Department rather than HUD; and despite its growing success, Treasury wanted the program killed, claiming it cost too much in foregone revenues. HUD Secretary Jack Kemp supported the program. An even more controversial program was a provision allowing the states to sell tax-free bonds and use the proceeds to help moderate- and low-income first-time home buyers. Both of these new approaches are being scrutinized closely as Congress and the president continue to wrestle with the mounting federal deficit.

If anything positive came from the savings and loan bailout, it may well have been the side effect that as a part of the S&L legislative package—a 1,000-page monster—Congress included provisions addressing housing and community development. Federal Home Loan Banks were required to provide financing for low-income housing. The measure also directed the Resolution Trust Corporation (RTC), charged with liquidating the foreclosed S&L-held properties, to give state and local governments and nonprofit organizations first chance at buying homes and apartment buildings. The legislation further mandated the 12 Federal Home Loan Banks across the country to establish special funds to subsidize interest rates on mortgages for low-income home buyers. Because their past performance in aiding low-income buyers has been only mediocre, the Home Loan Banks and S&Ls were subjected to strengthened reporting requirements on low-income loans. These provisions could generate more credit for home buyers and more funding for the development of low-income housing. Encouraging signs in February 1991 were a 16.4% growth in construction, an increase in building permit applications for the first time in 8 months, and a 7.9% increase in the sales of new homes. These figures marked the biggest rise in 5 years.

With the exception of these last programs mentioned, housing programs are for the most part under the supervision of HUD. Headquartered in a building some have described as "11 floors of basement," HUD employs about 17,000 people, only 4,700 of whom work in the Washington, D.C., offices. The remaining employees are spread among 10 regional offices and 81 other local offices across the country. In pursuing its primary mission of assuring suitable housing for all citizens, HUD has the responsibility for rehabilitation loans, urban homesteading, mortgage insurance, public housing, rent subsidies, mortgage subsidies, and community services for tenants. The Community Development Corporation, which administers Community Development Block Grants and other Community Development programs, and the Government National Mortgage Association, which purchases home mortgages from lending institutions to provide them more capital for home loans, are under HUD's direction.

The 1980s brought drastic reductions in HUD's budget as it plunged from $35.7 billion in 1980 to $15 billion in 1988. In 1980 HUD accounted for 7% of federal spending and by 1987 this had dipped to only 1% (Steinbach & Peirce, 1987). Under Ronald Reagan HUD experienced the severest budget cuts of any cabinet department. Adding to its woes, HUD was under investigation in the early 1990s for gross mismanagement and fraud in several of its programs under former secretary Samuel Pierce.

Conclusion

In the decades following World War II, the housing industry was a significant element in the national economy. Housing policies developed during that period were a combination of welfare and pork barrel programs. These efforts produced an alliance of homeowners, builders, and financial, banking, and interest groups that became a potent lobbying force. For evidence of their clout one need look no further than the mortgage interest deduction on federal income taxes, which costs the government over $30 billion in foregone revenues annually; efforts to repeal this write-off are doomed almost as soon as presented. During the first years of his administration, Ronald Reagan was able to counter these forces and cut federal housing expenditures quite deeply, but his efforts ran aground during his second term and the pendulum began to swing the other way. W. Donald Campbell, staff director for the Senate Subcommittee on Housing and Urban Affairs, said, "There's a growing feeling among a broad range of interest groups that things have gone too far" (Steinbach & Peirce, 1987, p. 1467).

With federal housing expenditures cut by 70% since 1980; housing assistance to the poor reduced to less than 10% of the annual housing budget; two thirds of those eligible for housing assistance getting no help; and the possible loss of as many as 1.5 million privately owned, federally subsidized low-rent housing units by 1995, Congress began to demonstrate a new aggressiveness on the issue of housing. Senator Alan Cranston (D., CA), chairman of the Subcommittee on Housing and Urban Affairs, stated, "There's a growing national consensus—a groundswell, in fact—in support of a new national housing policy" (Steinbach & Peirce, 1987, p. 1465). "Housing," Cranston said, "has been on the defensive all too long. It is time to end the federal government's hostility to housing and build an effective national policy" (p. 1464).

Along with the revival of interest in new housing efforts, there was also a widening recognition that some of the earlier programs were probably ill conceived from the start, others may have outlived their usefulness, and in a number of instances the primary beneficiaries were speculators, builders, developers, financiers, and the construction industry, who frequently reaped windfalls from federal housing projects. So even the proponents of new initiatives on the housing front do not expect a return to the large-scale federal spending of the decades prior to the 1980s. The White House's projected budgets propose modest increases in federal housing assistance through 1995 (see Figure 4.2).

With the national deficit placing constraints on any new federal spending initiatives, most observers saw new efforts to address the nation's housing problems as necessarily embracing a partnership approach. The private sector along with states and cities are likely to

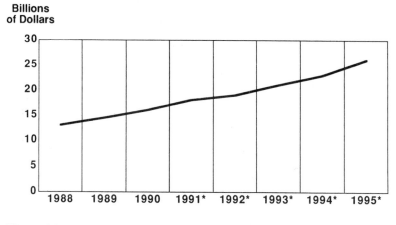

Figure 4.2. Federal Housing Assistance, 1988-1995
* Estimated
SOURCE: Budget of the United States.

become significant partners joining with the federal government in future efforts. This pattern has already been used in some areas under the tax credit provisions of the 1986 Tax Reform Act, as was described earlier. Other methods for encouraging such cooperative efforts will be necessary to meet the nation's growing housing needs. David Rosen (1989) of the National Center for Policy Alternatives, among others, has suggested, "A national housing trust is needed to assure steady revenues for construction and preservation of affordable, large-scale housing." Other approaches that have been suggested include a national lease-purchase plan for new homeowners, a national employer-assisted housing program, a program of individual housing accounts (IHAs) patterned on IRAs, and the offering of housing as an in-kind benefit as a part of income maintenance. Some advocates want housing for low-income persons made an entitlement program. They maintain that this approach would enable many more poor households to afford the rent for vacant units presently available (Steinbach, 1990a, p. 571). Whatever approaches are embraced, new housing policies will need to address both growth and replacement and will require long-term commitments. And, as the Brookings Institution fellow Anthony Downs pointed out, "There are no inexpensive ways to solve the nation's housing problems" (Steinbach, 1989, p. 855).

5

Jobs: Protection, Promotion, Training, Assistance

Americans traditionally have demonstrated a strong belief in the work ethic and self-sufficiency, and consequently, much of our social welfare policy is tied to working. For most of the early history of our country, employment was considered almost exclusively a private matter between the employer and his employees. Toward the end of the 19th century, some states began to adopt policies addressing the safety and health of workers, but the national government continued to follow largely a hands-off position in such matters.

The national government did adopt a limited 8-hour workday law in 1892, but not until the Great Depression and the New Deal did federal involvement expand to address a wide range of job-related activities. From that time to the present, the federal government has adopted policies ranging from the regulation of wages and hours through job training and creation, worker health and safety, and protection against unemployment to efforts to ensure equal employment opportunity for all workers.

Early efforts addressed four basic problems relative to employment: protecting the health, safety, and economic security of workers, especially women and children; protecting the right of workers to organize and bargain collectively with employers; providing sufficient employment opportunities in times of economic recession; and providing insurance protection during times of unemployment. These initial efforts were followed by policies designed to improve the employability and earning capacity of workers through education and skills training, especially among the poor or disadvantaged, and policies to protect certain categories of workers from employer discrimination. In seeking such a broad spectrum of employment goals through governmental action, it was impossible not to generate considerable controversy.

Major Issues

Some of the early efforts to regulate working conditions, wages, hours, use of child labor, and so forth were opposed by many on the grounds that such actions by government violated the employer's freedom to contract with employees regarding the terms of their employment and deprived employers of their property without due process of law.[1]

Another debate centers around whether governmental efforts should be directed toward generating more jobs in the private sector or providing public employment for those who cannot find jobs with private employers. Republicans tend to favor tax incentives and other programs designed to stimulate private sector employment, whereas Democrats are more willing to look to the public sector to provide jobs for the unemployed and hard to employ. The supporters of public employment maintain that many of the hard-core unemployed find it extremely difficult to find jobs in the private sector because they usually lack the skills private employers are looking for. They point out that although there may be jobs listed in the want ads, the available workers and the jobs many times do not match.

This is the reason for another group of programs that also meets with mixed responses. One of the reasons many workers cannot find jobs, work in jobs that provide only poverty-level wages, or are constantly in and out of the job market is because they lack the education and skills to compete effectively in the job market. Since the 1940s the federal government has launched a variety of programs designed to help the unemployed and the hard-to-employ improve their job skills and their chances for employment and career improvement. Such programs are costly, have produced mixed results, and tend to come in for considerable criticism. Some, such as the GI Bill, are regarded as great successes, whereas others, such as the Comprehensive Employment Training Act (CETA) and the Job Corps, are viewed by many conservatives as a waste of money. These critics point out that a person could attend college for less money than some employment training programs cost per trainee. Also such programs often have high dropout rates and trainees may have a hard time finding suitable jobs when they complete the programs.

Because they perceive social assistance programs such as AFDC, food stamps, and disability benefits as disincentives for recipients to work, most conservatives favor tying job training and employment programs to these assistance programs in what has been called workfare. Those who are physically able to work would have to participate in job training and employment programs to retain their eligibility for benefits under the other programs. The idea is that by forcing those able to work into these programs the welfare rolls will be reduced as they find jobs and become self-supporting. The problem with the workfare approach, its critics claim, is that many of those receiving benefits are unable to work and therefore cannot participate in the program. In 1987 interviews with more than 200 nonworkers by the Coalition on Human Needs revealed that more than half were hampered from going to work because of their age, poor health, child care costs, or absence of the necessary job skills. A recent study by Child Trends, a nonprofit Washington, D.C., think tank, found that typical welfare mothers were poorly educated, with lower than average learning skills, little work experience, and low self-esteem, and many suffered from depression. The study concluded that many welfare mothers have such tremendous educational, emotional, and intellectual deficits that they will never attain jobs paying enough to raise them out of poverty. Because almost all welfare mothers lack a college education, the jobs they are likely to get will be among those with the lowest pay ("Plan to free welfare moms from poverty lags," 1991). Often single parents working in minimum wage jobs do not even earn enough to cover day care costs for their children. Will Constable, regional director of the Child Service Division of the Kentucky Department of Social Services, observed: "It's not uncommon for a single mom working a minimum-wage job to spend more for day care than what she makes and it's very discouraging to parents to face that kind of a situation" (Purcell, 1991, p. 6-A).

Breaking the "welfare cycle" will require more than job training contend those who question the workfare concept. Job training will be futile unless there are jobs available for those who participate—jobs at wage levels that will make it worthwhile to go to work. Such a program will also require other forms of support to make it feasible: affordable child care for those who need it, some medical services if the employer does not provide them, and probably for many financial counseling, family counseling, and similar support services. Because workfare programs initially have not included provisions for such broad-based services, critics such as Andrew Dobelstein (1990) feel they have only "limited potential for assisting AFDC parents and their children." For those who have little employment potential, he wrote, the program has no meaning. Jason DeParle (1991) concluded workfare is a tougher, more expensive goal than most people realize. Such programs also do not have a good track record in the participants being able to find jobs. Most states limit participation in such programs to 2 years, and for many participants this frequently is not long enough to solve their problems and make them employable. One 1980 study by the Manpower Demonstration Research Corporation found that only 7%-10% of those who participated in such programs found steady jobs. Workfare and job training alone address only a part of the problem of helping break the welfare dependency of many. (See "Workfare" section, pp. 91-92.)

Probably one of the most controversial areas relative to federal policies on employment in recent years has been that of equal opportunity and affirmative action. In an effort to compensate for past patterns of discrimination against certain classes of prospective workers, the government has put in place policies designed to encourage the recruitment and hiring of more persons in these categories. Because such policies inevitably work to the advantage of some and to the disadvantage of others, they have become quite controversial. Conservative critics of these efforts charge that they have gone beyond equal opportunity and in many instances constitute reverse discrimination. Some critics contend that the government has inserted itself into the employment field to such an extent that it requires employers to hire and promote a number of employees in certain categories whether they are qualified or not. Liberal proponents of such policies maintain that in their absence, employers and the job market would eliminate such inequities very slowly, if at all.

Efforts at Solution

Prior to the Great Depression and the New Deal, the federal government made only minimal efforts to regulate the job market and even these efforts frequently encountered problems in the courts. The massive unemployment and widespread economic hardship experienced by the country's workers during the Great Depression changed this pattern dramatically. President Roosevelt's New Deal produced a flood of worker-related legislation directed at a wide array of problems. In 1931 Congress enacted the Davis-Bacon Act, requiring employers receiving federal contracts to pay their employees the prevailing wage for the area where the work was being done in an effort to ensure workers were paid a fair wage and cheap labor was not imported from another area to the detriment of the local economy. In 1936 Congress passed the Walsh-Healey Act, which prohibited employers working under federal contracts from using child labor and established minimum wage and maximum hours requirements for their employees. Two years later Congress extended wages and hours regulation with the passage of the Fair Labor Standards Act. Aimed at eliminating substandard working conditions, this act established a minimum wage of 25 cents per hour and a maximum workweek of 44 hours for workers employed in businesses engaged in interstate commerce. The act prohibited the employment of children under 16 years of age in such businesses (making more jobs available for unemployed older workers), and those under 18 years of age were restricted to employment in nonhazardous jobs. The minimum wage advanced to 30 cents per hour in 1939 and the workweek dropped to 40 hours in 1940. The immediate impact of the act when it took effect was to give 750,000 workers a wage increase. Passage of the act marked a shift from the "cost of living" concept of wages to a "fair value" concept (*Congress and the Nation,* 1965, p. 636).

Although the minimum wage has been periodically adjusted by Congress over the years, it has not kept pace with either economic growth rates or inflation rates (see Table 5.1). Real earnings per worker have not grown for over 15 years in the United States (Aaron, 1990; Wicker, 1991). In 1988 the minimum wage earner had an income of $6,968, which was $4,644 below the official poverty level for a family of four. The poverty level for a single person was $5,574. During the 1980s the number of workers moonlighting (holding more than one job) doubled, rising to 6.2%. Women accounted for much of this increase with 3.2 million females holding at least two jobs in 1989; 66% of the increase in moonlighting from 1985 to 1989 was due to females taking additional jobs (see Clark, 1987b; Steinbach, 1990b). Because many jobs do not pay as well as in the past, more and more workers find it difficult to live on only one salary.

Table 5.1 Minimum Wage Rates, 1938-1991

1938-39	$ .25	1974	2.00
1939-45	.30	1975	2.10
1945-50	.40	1976-77	2.30
1950-56	.75	1978	2.65
1956-61	1.00	1979	2.90
1961-63	1.15	1980	3.10
1963-67	1.25	1981-89	3.35
1967-68	1.40	1990	3.85
1968-74	1.60	1991	4.25

Since the last increase in the minimum wage was in 1981, Congress decided in the late 1980s that an increase was overdue. Senator Edward Kennedy (D., MA), chairman of the Senate Labor and Public Welfare Committee, observed: "The minimum wage is not a living wage, and it is not a decent society in which a full-time job means a lifetime of poverty" (Clark 1987b, p. 702). Kennedy was joined by others who felt the wage needed adjusting. Congressman Thomas J. Downey (D., NY) said, "Our concern is that people who work should not be poor" (Kosterlitz 1989c, p. 1111). The labor lobbyist Arnold Mayer pointed out, "There are millions of people out there who work like hell and can't afford to raise their families" (Clark 1987b, p. 705). Others, including the U.S. Chamber of Commerce and President Bush, opposed an increase. They claimed any increase would raise unemployment levels by causing employers to lay off workers; would result in fewer new jobs, especially for younger people; and would contribute to inflation. Despite strong opposition, in 1989 Congress passed a bill increasing the minimum wage; President Bush vetoed it. Congress then passed a second measure with lower increases spread over 2 years and a provision for a subminimum "training wage" for new employees, which President Bush accepted. Under the new law the wage rose to $3.85 per hour in 1990 and $4.25 in 1991. These changes brought slight increases for a number of workers. In 1987 about 12.5 million workers earned $4.00 per hour or less and another 10 million earned $4.00-$5.00 per hour (Clark, 1987b, p. 705). These increases still raised minimum wage earners only to near or barely above the poverty level. Many feel the 1989 bill did not do enough; budget constraints make further increases difficult.

Collective Bargaining

In efforts to improve the bargaining power of workers for better wages and working conditions, the New Deal took steps to ensure employees the right to bargain collectively with employers. In 1932 Congress passed the Norris-LaGuardia Act, which outlawed "yellow-dog" contracts in which workers had to agree not to join a union or engage in efforts to form one and imposed limits on the use of injunctions in labor disputes. In 1935 came the National Labor Relations Act, or Wagner Act, which guaranteed employees' rights to organize and bargain collectively with employers. With the passage of these two measures, union membership and political and economic influence grew rapidly. Using their collective bargaining powers the unions were able to secure better wages and working conditions in many industries. Following World War II, union activities and their growing power resulted in a backlash, which produced the Taft-Hartley Act in 1947 and the Landrum-Griffin Act in 1959. Reflecting growing antiunion sentiment, these bills imposed restrictions on the unions, their leaders, and their activities. Since the early 1960s the unions have been fighting a sort of holding action to protect the wages and benefits achieved in more favorable economic times.

Public Employment

Much of the New Deal effort was directed toward providing employment and income for those forced out of work by the depression. New Deal relief efforts were launched with the creation in 1933 of the Civilian Conservation Corps (CCC), a program to help unemployed young men from needy families by putting them to work on conservation projects planting trees, building dams, and so forth. This was followed by the establishment that same year of the Public Works Administration (PWA) to increase employment and expand consumer spending by providing jobs in public construction projects. Under the PWA program thousands of new schools, courthouses, bridges, dams, and other projects were built. Two other programs were added in 1935. The National Youth Administration was created to provide job training for unemployed youths and part-time work for needy students. The Works Progress Administration (WPA) provided jobs for the unemployed building highways, streets, bridges, parks, public buildings, and the like. This program also provided employment for artists, writers, actors, and musicians. A major thrust of these programs was to stimulate economic recovery by providing workers gainful employment and increasing their spending power. Although the efforts were far reaching—the WPA alone provided work for about 8.5 million persons—there were still 7.5 million unemployed in 1940 and it took World War II to bring full economic recovery (*Congress and the Nation,* 1965). But the ice had been broken and the precedent set for governmental efforts to provide jobs and training for those out of work.

Unemployment Insurance

Although not exclusively a program for workers, social security was strongly supported by organized labor and provided various benefits for workers and their families. The unemployment insurance provisions of the program were designed to provide income assistance for those who were temporarily out of work. This section of the Social Security Act provided a federal tax incentive for the states to establish their own programs, which were administered by the individual states under federal guidelines. Because the programs are state administered and partially state financed, benefit levels and duration of benefits vary from state to state. In 1989 the typical unemployed worker got about $150 per week in benefits, or approximately 40% of normal employment income; benefits ranged from $259 per week in Nebraska to only $105 per week in Indiana (*World Almanac,* 1990, p. 135). Typically such benefits last only a few months and often expire before a worker finds a new job. Even the highest benefit levels would still leave recipients below the official poverty level even when food stamps are included.

World War II ended the high unemployment rates of the depression years and the 1950s and 1960s had relatively low unemployment levels, averaging about 4.6%. As economic growth slowed, these rates climbed to over 6% in the 1970s and close to 8% in the 1980s (see Figure 5.1 and Table 5.2). During the 1982 recession the unemployment rate hit 10.8%, the highest level since the early 1940s, and in early 1991, with the economy again in a slump, 7.7 million, or 7.1% were unemployed (Van Horn et al., 1989; "State jobless rate fell to 7.3% in April," 1991). Average figures for unemployment tend to understate the problem, however. The official Department of Labor figures do not reflect those who have become discouraged and are no longer seeking employment, nor do they take into consideration those who are working only part-time but would prefer full-time employment. Over the last decade more

Percent

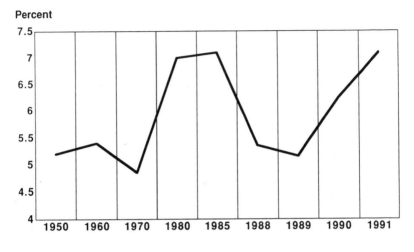

Figure 5.1. Unemployment Patterns, 1950-1991
SOURCE: U.S. Bureau of Labor Statistics, *Monthly Labor Review.*

and more employers have been turning to part-time employees, because they are cheaper. The median wage for part-timers in 1987 was $4.42 per hour compared to $7.43 per hour for full-timers. Not only are part-timers cheaper in pay, they also cost employers much less in fringe benefits. Most get limited or no benefits. Also part-time workers are disproportionately concentrated in lower-paying operations. Although many work part-time by choice, others would prefer full-time employment. The Economic Policy Institute reported that at least one quarter of those working only part-time in 1988 preferred to work full-time. The institute also found that women, blacks, and teenagers were much more likely to be working only part-time against their wishes. In 1988, 18.4% of the work force was part-time, but 27% of women in the work force were part-time. Women were 1.5 times as likely to work only part-time as were all participants and 1.2 times as likely to be working part-time against their wishes. Blacks and teenagers were twice as likely to have only part-time jobs even when they preferred full-time employment ("Making ends meet with part-time work," 1990).

Employment statistics also gloss over other dramatic variations from the norm. Unemployment varies significantly from region to region; some states have rates double the national average and some urban area

Table 5.2 Unemployment Rates by Age, Race, Sex

Marital Status, Race, and Age	Men				Women			
	Thousands of Persons		Unemployment Rates		Thousands of Persons		Unemployment Rates	
	Feb. 1990	Feb. 1991	Feb. 1990	Feb. 1991	Feb. 1990	Feb. 1991	Feb. 1990	Feb. 1991
Total, 16 years and over	4,087	5,427	6.1	8.0	3,047	3,491	5.4	6.2
Married, spouse present	1,573	2,161	3.7	5.1	1,232	1,432	4.0	4.6
Widowed, divorced, or separated	589	793	8.4	10.8	674	756	6.0	6.7
Single (never married)	1,925	2,474	10.7	13.6	1,140	1,303	8.2	9.3
White, 16 years and over	3,178	4,328	5.4	7.4	2,247	2,630	4.7	5.5
Married, spouse present	1,318	1,848	3.5	4.9	1,020	1,252	3.7	4.5
Widowed, divorced, or separated	447	630	7.6	10.4	498	565	5.6	6.2
Single (never married)	1,413	1,850	9.4	12.2	729	812	6.5	7.3
Black, 16 years and over	778	921	11.9	13.9	716	730	10.6	11.0
Married, spouse present	198	233	6.2	7.3	165	129	6.8	5.5
Widowed, divorced, or separated	125	145	13.3	13.9	162	166	8.1	8.8
Single (never married)	455	542	19.0	22.7	390	435	16.4	18.2
Total, 25 years and over	2,745	3,787	4.8	6.6	2,049	2,410	4.4	5.1
Married, spouse present	1,443	2,023	3.5	5.0	1,048	1,243	3.6	4.3
Widowed, divorced, or separated	573	764	8.4	10.8	613	696	5.6	6.4
Single (never married)	729	1,001	8.0	10.5	388	471	5.9	6.9
White, 25 years and over	2,144	3,065	4.3	6.1	1,510	1,864	3.9	4.7
Married, spouse present	1,206	1,727	3.3	4.8	878	1,085	3.4	4.2
Widowed, divorced, or separated	435	607	7.6	10.4	449	529	5.2	6.0
Single (never married)	503	732	6.8	9.4	183	250	3.7	4.9
Black, 25 years and over	509	590	9.5	10.8	475	479	8.6	8.7
Married, spouse present	180	222	5.9	7.2	125	115	5.6	5.1
Widowed, divorced, or separated	121	141	13.1	13.9	153	148	7.9	8.1
Single (never married)	208	227	15.3	16.6	196	216	14.2	15.1

SOURCE: U.S. Bureau of Labor Statistics, *Monthly Labor Review*.

rates are three times higher than the national average. Likewise, extremely high rates among certain categories of citizens are not reflected in these average figures. Young blacks and Hispanics, for example, both experience disproportionately high rates of unemployment (see Table 5.2).

Not only do unemployment benefits often expire before the unemployed worker finds a new job, many workers still are not covered by the program. The Reagan administration cutbacks in social program spending reduced unemployment insurance payments to the states, terminated the extended benefits portion of the program, and reduced the supplemental benefits segment. Consequently, at the height of the recession in the early 1980s, only about 45% of those unemployed were receiving benefits. This compared to 75% who where receiving benefits in 1975 (Bawden & Palmer, 1982). In 1988 an estimated 1.7 million unemployed were receiving benefits, or about one third (33%) of those unemployed. As we entered the 1990s with 7-8 million unemployed, benefits were at one of their lowest levels. According to the Center on Budget and Policy Priorities, during the first quarter of 1990, 37% of those who were unemployed drew benefits. From the end of World War II to 1983 the average of those receiving benefits dipped below 40% only once—in 1966—when it hit 39%. From 1984 to 1989 coverage dropped to record lows, averaging about 33%. Coverage has climbed gradually but could decline again as demands increase. For the week ending March 23, 1991, more people filed for benefits than at any time since 1983, increasing pressures on the system ("Unemployment protection said at unparalleled low," 1991). This trend caused John Sturdivant, president of the American Federation of Government Employees, to observe: "We seem to be able to mobilize the resources of our country for Desert Storm and bailing out the savings and loans, but we haven't been doing it for our unemployed workers" ("AFL-CIO proposes federal jobs program," 1991).

A somewhat similar program also provided jointly by the federal and state governments is **workers' compensation.** Compensation laws were first enacted by states in 1911 and by 1912 all but eight states had such programs. Today all 50 states have programs, but there are wide variations in administration and benefits state to state. In 1972 Congress established the National Commission on State Workmen's Compensation Laws to study the system. The commission reported that state programs in general were "inadequate and inequitable." It recommended that if improvements were not shown within 3 years, federal standards be set for these programs. The Carter administration considered further action, but none was taken. Several states have been hard pressed budgetarily as the costs of their workers' compensation programs have spiraled upward and employers have rebelled against higher contributions. This program provides benefits to workers who are injured on the job and temporarily unable to work. Nationwide in 1989 there were 9 million workplace-related injuries and illnesses, and benefits payments exceeded $40 billion (Victor, 1990b, p. 1537).

Job Training

One of the major factors contributing to unemployment and low wages is the lack of education and marketable job skills on the part of many prospective workers. Unemployment rates among the uneducated and unskilled are substantially above the national average, and during the 1970s and 1980s the earnings of those least educated and least skilled have declined the most. Job opportunities for uneducated and unskilled workers are continually shrinking.

Since World War II the federal government has put in place a host of policies and programs aimed at improving the education, skills, and employability of prospective workers. Though not purely a jobs training program, the 1944 GI Bill provided educational and training support for the soldiers returning from the war to help ease their transition into the civilian work force. This program served a dual purpose of keeping all the returning soldiers from entering the job market all at once, thus creating a job crunch, and enabling them to improve their educational and skills levels and ultimately their employability and earning power. This effort was a marked success and ultimately benefited the government through increased revenues resulting from the increased taxes paid by the program's beneficiaries as a result of their improved earning power.

Despite the success of the GI Bill, many conservatives continue to harbor strong reservations about governmental job training programs and such concerns are not without some cause. Such programs frequently have been without clear focus, have been laxly and poorly administered, and have failed to produce results commensurate to their costs. Because they deal with elements of the population that have largely been excluded by the social and economic systems, they are high-risk efforts and limited success, though often criticized, is probably the most that realistically should be expected. Therefore, even though these programs remain controversial, national policymakers continue to believe that one of the most effective methods for fighting poverty is through programs designed to get more of the disadvantaged into the labor market.

The 1950s and 1960s were a period of relatively sustained economic growth and low unemployment rates. In 1960 John F. Kennedy came to the White House with a pledge to "get the country moving again." In 1962 he convinced Congress to pass the Manpower Development and Training Act (MDTA), the first comprehensive effort by the federal government to help the unemployed and underemployed secure training in skills needed for jobs available in the market. Under President Johnson the program was expanded and the emphasis was shifted to training for younger persons with little or no work experience. In 1966 amendments, Congress directed that 65% of the effort go for training the hard-core unemployed and 35% for training in skills in short supply in the job market. More than 1 million persons were enrolled in MDTA programs, with 600,000 completing their first courses. Seventy-five percent got jobs at the end of their program.

As a part of the War on Poverty, Johnson proposed several new initiatives on the job training front. Probably the most controversial of all Office of Economic Opportunity (OEO) programs was the Job Corps. The Job Corps takes unemployed and poorly educated youths, mostly high school dropouts, to residential conservation camp training centers. Run by private contractors, these centers provide 2-year programs, including basic education courses and job training. The purpose is to remove the youths from their troubled home environment for 2 years and provide them with counseling and marketable job skills in an effort to make them contributing members of society. Riots and incidents of violence at several camps and high dropout rates, coupled with what many perceived as unduly high costs per trainee, led to widespread early criticism of the program. But Congress kept pushing for tighter administration of the program and in 1967 the House Education and Labor Committee reported: "We are convinced that the Job Corps is making a significant contribution towards eradication of poverty" (*Congress and the Nation,* 1969, p. 749).

A strong advocate for the Job Corps is Carl T. Rowan, former director of the U.S. Information Agency under President Kennedy and now a liberal nationally syndicated columnist. Rowan (1991) sees the Job Corps as a major success, pointing out that in more than 20 years over 1.5 million troubled youths have been prepared for jobs at a success rate of 84 per 100 enrolled. He sees the Corps, whose trainees are 53% black,

31% white, 11% Hispanic, 3% Native American and 2% Asian-Pacific, as successful but underfunded. Of 5 million impoverished youth nationwide, 441,000 "seriously at risk," only 68,000 or about 2% will get a chance to participate in the program. Rowan contrasts the budget for the Job Corps with that of the U.S. Bureau of Prisons—$1.16 billion for the corps for FY 1992 and twice that amount for the bureau. The bureau requested $314 million to build prison space for 3600 new beds, a cost of $87,000 per bed. Too few Americans and their leaders, charges Rowan, seem to realize that our resources would be better spent on education, jobs, and training than incarceration.

Also included in OEO's work training programs were the Neighborhood Youth Corps, Summer Youth Employment Program, Operation Mainstream, and New Careers. The Neighborhood Youth Corps program provided federal assistance to state and local programs that provided work for underprivileged youths on projects beneficial to their communities. Operation Mainstream, added in 1965, provided jobs for the chronically unemployed working on community beautification projects. New Careers, added in 1966, was to provide training for the poor to become aides to various professionals—teachers, librarians, and the like. Under President Nixon several of these programs were combined and shifted from OEO to the Department of Labor as he took steps to dismantle OEO.

Many of the existing job training efforts were combined in 1973 under the Comprehensive Employment Training Act (CETA) umbrella. CETA marked the first step in the direction of workfare, combining income maintenance and job training support. Participants were provided income while enrolled in job training courses. The act included funds for skills training, counseling, remedial education, subsidized employment, and job creation. Although its goals and comprehensive approach were commendable, CETA foundered on a host of administrative problems. Because most of the field staff lacked experience in employment training, local sponsors of training programs were allowed broad discretion in running their programs. An array of locally based interest groups developed to push the cause of local CETA programs. Local sponsors, often units of local government and public agencies, "skimmed" the most talented from the pool of potential trainees, thus blunting two prime objectives of the program: serving the disadvantaged and preparing persons for private sector employment. In many areas public agencies used CETA funds to increase their own staffs. Largely because of poor administration, too much of CETA funding was spent on income maintenance and too little on skill training, job creation, and private sector placement. Consequently, CETA encountered growing criticism and was replaced in 1982 with the Job Training and Partnership Act (JTPA).

The major purpose of the JTPA was "to prepare youth and unskilled adults for entry into the labor force and to afford job training to those economically disadvantaged individuals and other individuals facing serious barriers to employment, who are in special need of such training to obtain productive employment." The major difference between JTPA and earlier programs was its greater intent to involve the private sector as a part of the solution to the employment problem. The instrument for doing this was to be local Private Industry Councils (PICs) made up of representatives from local businesses and industries. Council members would be chosen by local officials, and the local PICs would develop the job training programs, decide what services needed to be provided, and then enter into contracts with private training providers. The states are charged with ensuring that the PICs and the training providers meet performance standards, and as the program has evolved, the states have increasingly assumed the responsibility for oversight, causing some concern that once again the objective of reaching those who need help most is not being achieved. Part of the problem stems from a lack of clear direction and the fact that the program is administered in such a way that it seeks to serve conflicting constituencies. The way the law is written and the program administered encourages "creaming": The training contractors are paid on the basis of their success in placing people in jobs quickly and the employers are seeking the best workers to fill their available positions. Consequently, both are looking for the most trainable and capable potential workers and these usually are not those most in need. Jeff Faux, president of the Economic Policy Institute, said that under JTPA there was "an obsession with very, very short-term goals—placing people very quickly in jobs they would have gotten anyway" (Victor, 1990a). Harvard Professor John Donahue concluded the JTPA had failed to attain its goal of reducing waste in federal job training and helping those who most need employment. Because the private training approach emphasizes short-term employment of those most easily trained, the program largely fails to touch those most in need of help ("Infofile," 1990a, p. 807). Sar A. Levitan of George Washington University's Center for Social Policy Studies argued that there are mistakes, but concluded "It is certainly a program that is greatly needed" (Victor, 1990a, p. 900). The Inspector General's report on JTPA stated that after seven years no one knew exactly what the return on investment was (p. 900). For FY 1991 Congress appropriated $3.76 billion for JTPA, an increase of $318 million.

Workfare

During the Reagan years there was a growing acceptance of the idea that welfare assistance should be tied to jobs. This "workfare" concept was incorporated into the 1986 welfare reform legislation as Job Opportunities and Basic Skills (JOBS). Under this new program the states are required to enroll at least 20% of their public assistance cases in job training by 1995. Aid recipients who refuse to participate will forfeit part of their benefits. The program's objective is to reduce the numbers on welfare by providing them marketable skills and moving them into the work force.

As the states geared up to meet the 1995 deadline, many saw the obstacles to the program's success as substantial. In the first place, they pointed out, many of those on the welfare rolls are not physically able to go to work because of poor health, age, or disability. Furthermore, noted the skeptics, most research indicates that mandatory work programs have proven ineffective in moving people off of welfare and into the work force (Chisman & Pifer, 1987; Dobelstein, 1990; Manpower Demonstration Research Corporation, 1980). The jobs usually available to these types of workers pay low wages, provide few fringe benefits, require hard physical work, and in many cases are only seasonal or part-time. One welfare recipient commenting on the program observed, "I can't see them training us for anything but $4-an-hour jobs." With two or three children, "You can't live off that." "Where are the jobs?" she asked (Lawson, 1990, p. A1).

What do you do, asked the skeptics, when those who leave the welfare rolls to go to work still cannot earn their way out of poverty? Under current programs and policies those receiving welfare benefits who go to work can expect two things: When their earnings reach a certain level, they will have to start paying income taxes, and they will also see their welfare benefits reduced dollar for dollar as their earnings rise. For those shifting from welfare to work, effective marginal tax rates (that is, the portion of their earnings that end up going to the government) as high as 80% are not unusual. This compares to 33% for those in the upper income brackets, a rate many, including President Bush, consider excessive. Add to this the loss of medicaid and the costs of child care and transportation, and many persons end up keeping little or none of the money they earn by going to work. For persons in these circumstances the rewards from work are seldom greater than the costs. These are some of the reasons many feel workfare is doomed to fail unless accompanied by other efforts that will generate jobs that make it worthwhile for people to go to work. Evidence indicates that when well-paying jobs are available, people are eager to go to work (Burtless, 1989; Dobelstein, 1990).

Equal Employment Opportunity

Though most Americans express strong belief in the concepts of equality and fair treatment for all, the objective of equal rights enunci- ated in such basic documents as the Declaration of Independence, the Bill of Rights, and the Fourteenth Amendment has been more idea than reality. In 1873 in *Bradwell v. Illinois,* the U.S. Supreme Court upheld a state law prohibiting women from practicing law, and as recently as 1961 in *Hoyt v. Florida* the Court upheld a state law providing women could serve on juries only if they volunteered for such duty. In *Bradwell,* Justice Joseph Bradley offered this observation on a woman's role: "The paramount destiny and mission of woman are to fulfill the noble and benign offices of wife and mother. This is the law of the Creator" (p. 141). In the 1973 decision in *Frontiero v. Richardson,* Justice Wil- liam Brennan noted that in the past: "Neither slaves nor women could hold office, serve on juries, or bring suits in their own names, and married women traditionally were denied the legal capacity to hold or convey property or to serve as legal guardians of their own children" (p. 685). Clearly full social and economic equality had not been achieved for all in our society. One of the areas where such discrimination was most persistent was in the area of employment.

Still after several decades of governmental efforts to overcome em- ployment discrimination, minorities and females have not gained social and economic equality. In 1988, 11.9% of black families and 8.4% of Hispanic families had incomes of less than $5,000; for white families the comparable figure was 3.0%. At the other end of the scale, 27.4% of white families had incomes of $50,000 or more whereas only 12.6% of black families and 11.9% of Hispanic families had incomes in excess of $50,000. Black family income is about 57%-58% of that for white families; for Hispanics the figure is about 65%, and the income of female-headed families is about 60% of that of a family headed by a

Table 5.3 Income of Individuals by Race and Spanish Origin, 1980-1987

	White		Black		Spanish Origin	
	1980	*1987*	*1980*	*1987*	*1980*	*1987*
Median Income						
Male	$19,719	$27,468	$13,874	$19,385	$13,790	$17,872
Female	11,702	17,775	10,914	16,211	9,887	14,893
Median Family						
Income	$21,904	$32,274	$12,674	$18,098	$14,717	$20,306
Percentage of Families With Income:						
Less than $10,000	16.2%	9.3%	40.4%	29.4%	32.3%	22.9%
$15,000-25,000	28.3	18.4	23.0	21.8	26.2	21.9
$25,000 and over	41.6	62.7	19.8	35.9	22.8	40.5
Percentage of Persons						
Below the Poverty Line	10.2%	10.5%	32.5%	33.1%	25.7%	28.2%

NOTE: For all persons over 15 years old who had income.
SOURCE: U.S. Bureau of the Census (1990).

single male. On the average, blacks and females earn about 65%-70% of what white males earn (see Table 5.3). In 1987 the median income for female workers was $16,909 and for men the figure was $26,008; about two thirds of the females in the work force earned less than $13,000 (Navarro, 1984, ch. 10; Wilson, 1990; U.S. Bureau of the Census, 1990, pp. 450-451). Part of the problem stems from the types of jobs minorities and females are concentrated in. Over 50% of all white workers are in white-collar jobs whereas only about 35% of blacks are in such jobs. In the South about two thirds of black employees are in unskilled or semiskilled low-status, low-paying jobs (Navarro, 1984). For women job segregation is a major factor in their pay inequity. Whereas male employees are widely distributed across over 200 occupations, 50% of all female workers are concentrated in only 21 occupations. A number of these occupations are almost exclusively female and traditionally pay less than occupations including mostly males (Navarro, 1984; see Tables 5.4 and 5.5).

Even when minority and female workers have been able to improve their type of employment, they continue to encounter discrimination in the workplace. Blacks in the skilled trades, for example, earn on the average about 70% of what whites in these positions earn. In managerial, administrative, and sales positions, black males earn about 65% of what whites in these positions earn, and blacks in professional and

Table 5.4 Distribution of Female Workers by Jobs Held

Job	% of Women in Field
Clerical	35.0
Service	17.2
Professional/technical	16.1
Machine operators	11.5
Sales	6.9
Managerial-household	6.4
Private-household	2.6
Craft	1.8
Laborer (nonfarm)	1.3
Worker (farm)	1.2

SOURCE: From *The American Almanac of Jobs and Salaries* by John Wright and Edward Dwyer, p. 568. Copyright © 1990 by John Wright and Edward Dwyer. Published by arrangement with Avon Books, a division of the Hearst Corporation. Reprinted with permission.

technical fields are paid about 70% as much as their white counterparts (Wright & Dwyer, 1990, pp. 573-575). Although females have improved their job status over the last decade, they still experience similar

Table 5.5 Jobs Filled Primarily by Women

Field	% Women
Secretary	97.7
Receptionist	97.6
Telephone operator	92.9
Typist	96.6
Keypunch operator	95.6
Dental assistant	98.0
Registered nurse	96.0
Practical nurse	97.0
Waitress	90.0
Bank teller	93.5
Billing clerk	88.1
Bookkeeper	90.7
Cashier	86.2
File clerk	85.7

SOURCE: From *The American Almanac of Jobs and Salaries* by John Wright and Edward Dwyer, p. 568. Copyright © 1990 by John Wright and Edward Dwyer. Published by arrangement with Avon Books, a division of the Hearst Corporation. Reprinted with permission.

patterns of job discrimination. From 1970 to 1980 the number of women in management positions rose from 10% to 19% and in professional positions from 25% to 38%. Between 1975 and 1985 the numbers of females in law rose from 7.1% to 18.2%. But despite these advances, only about 1% of those in the upper echelons of management are female. Over two thirds of the top 1,300 U.S. corporations have no females on their boards of directors, and female CEOs of *Fortune* 500 companies are virtually nonexistent (Navarro, 1984). Even with more women entering professions such as law and accounting, few become full partners in the major firms.

These patterns of racial and sexual discrimination are deeply rooted in U.S. history and culture and do not yield easily to efforts to change them. Concerted efforts through the civil rights and women's movements have brought increased government involvement and some improvement, however. In 1961 President Kennedy appointed a special commission on the status of women chaired by Eleanor Roosevelt. A major concern of the commission, which made its report in 1963, was the inequity experienced by women in the workplace. That same year Congress passed the Equal Pay Act, requiring employers to grant equal pay for equal work regardless of an employee's sex. Many employers had used different job titles and pay scales for male and female employees even though the work performed was the same. The following year Congress put in place the keystone of federal employment policy—Title VII of the Civil Rights Act of 1964. Title VII prohibits employers from discriminating against employees based on their race, national origin, sex, or religion. Interestingly, sex was added as a category under the bill by Southern congressmen in an effort to kill the measure. It was passed anyway. This legislation also created the Equal Employment Opportunity Commission (EEOC), which, along with the Office of Federal Contract Compliance programs and the Civil Rights Division of the Department of Justice, administers and enforces federal policies on equal employment opportunity.

President Johnson's Great Society concept included the acceptance of federal responsibility for broader efforts on behalf of those who were not afforded equal opportunity by the current system. What was not addressed through legislation, he did by executive order, putting in place a policy of affirmative action requiring a special effort by certain employers to recruit and hire those who had been victims of past patterns of discrimination. "Equal opportunity, he said, is essential, but not enough. We seek not just legal equity but human ability, not just equality as a right and a theory but equality as a fact and equality as a result."

Legislative efforts against discrimination also continued. In 1967 Congress passed the Age Discrimination Act to protect older employees from discriminatory hiring and firing practices. The Civil Rights Act of 1972 expanded EEOC authority by allowing it to file suits in the federal courts and extended the provisions of the Equal Employment Act to all businesses or unions with 15 or more members and state and local governments. In 1978 federal employees were added. Antidiscrimination clauses became commonplace in federal legislation in the 1970s, starting with Title IX of the 1972 Education Act Amendments and including the Comprehensive Employment and Training Act (1973), the Crime Control Act (1973), and the Disaster Relief Act (1974). In 1978 Congress passed the Pregnancy Discrimination Act protecting pregnant employees from discrimination by their employers.

In the 1970s and 1980s, with much of the debate focusing on affirmative action, the center of activity shifted from Congress to the courts. Because affirmative action required special treatment for certain categories of persons, those who saw themselves thereby displaced filed lawsuits charging that it constituted reverse discrimination. Much of the confusion surrounding affirmative action stemmed from a lack of clarity and understanding of what the laws and guidelines required. The Civil Rights Act of 1964 prohibited the use of "quotas," but affirmative action guidelines required the establishment of "goals" and "timetables." These were the issues the courts were called upon to clarify.

The landmark affirmative action case did not involve jobs, but a university's medical school admissions policy. In a 1978 decision in *University of California Regents v. Bakke* a 5-4 majority of the U.S. Supreme Court upheld the university's right to consider race as a factor in its admissions decisions but disallowed that part of the affirmative action plan that set aside a fixed number of positions for minorities, saying fixed quotas were not allowed under the law. The following year in *United Steelworkers of America v. Weber* a 5-2 majority of the Court upheld the Kaiser Company's affirmative action plan, which used separate lists and favored minority employees in the choosing of trainees for a newly created crafts program. The Court said voluntary affirmative action plans by private employers to compensate for past employment discrimination did not violate the 1964 Civil Rights Act or the Fourteenth Amendment. In *Fullilove v. Klutznick* (1980) the Court upheld a 10% set-aside for minority contractors on federal public works construction projects as a part of the minority business enterprise provision under amendments to the Public Works Employment Act of

1977. Although many critics felt this came awfully close to sanctioning quotas, the Court reaffirmed its position in 1990, upholding the FCC's policy favoring minorities in the awarding of broadcast licenses. Writing for the majority, Justice William Brennan stated: "We hold that benign race-conscious measures mandated by Congress—even if those measures are not remedial in the sense of being designed to compensate victims of past governmental or societal discrimination—are constitutionally permissible" (*Metro Broadcasting v. FCC,* 1990, p. 5066). The Court has also ruled that affirmative action is justified on behalf of minorities and females even when it would benefit persons not actual victims of discrimination themselves (*Local 28 of the Sheetmetal Workers International Assn. v. EEOC,* 1986). And in *Johnson v. Transportation Agency, Santa Clara County* (1987) the Court ruled that if women and minorities are underrepresented in the workplace, employers can take action to remedy such an imbalance.

Some feel that these decisions go beyond what is appropriate governmental effort. Justice Potter Stewart, dissenting in *Fullilove v. Klutznick* wrote:

> Under our Constitution, any official action that treats a person differently on account of his race or ethnic origin is inherently suspect and presumptively invalid. . . . The hostility of the Constitution to racial classifications by government has been manifested in many cases decided by this Court. . . . Under our Constitution the government may never act to the detriment of a person solely because of that person's race. (p. 523-525)

President Reagan's appointees to the Court have been frequent dissenters on affirmative action cases. In *Metro Broadcasting v. FCC* (1990), Justice Anthony Kennedy wrote: "I cannot agree with the Court that the Constitution permits the government to discriminate among its citizens on the basis of race in order to serve interests so trivial as broadcast diversity" (p. 5076).

Two elements that have plagued the Courts in addressing the issues of affirmative action and employment discrimination are those of discriminatory effect versus discriminatory intent and whether those who were not a party to the discrimination should be penalized in effect to compensate for something for which they were in no way responsible. In 1971 in *Griggs v. Duke Power Company,* the majority used the "disparate impact" or "discriminatory effect" concept to hold the company's recruitment and employment procedures discriminatory under the law.

The Court ruled that any tests or other screening devices used in the employment process that had the effect of eliminating higher proportions of certain categories of workers must be proven relevant to the performance of the job. But the Court has not always felt comfortable with this strict approach and has backed away from it in other cases. In 1984 in *Firefighters' Local Union 1784 v. Stotts* the Court held that a union's bona fide seniority system took precedence over the fire department's affirmative action plan and layoffs should be in accordance with the seniority plan regardless of race. The Court also said that persons not a party to discriminatory actions could not be deprived of their legal rights in efforts to atone for past patterns of discrimination. The Court took a similar position in *Wygant v. Jackson Board of Education* (1986), saying layoffs of whites who had not been a party to discrimination to achieve racial balance among employees was not justifiable. The Court moved even further away from the disparate impact concept of the *Griggs* case when it shifted the burden of proof in such discrimination cases from the employer to the complaining employee (*Wards Cove Packing Company v. Atonio,* 1989; see also *City of Richmond v. Croson,* 1989). In other words, if an employer claims that a hiring decision was based on business necessity, the employee or prospective employee must prove the employer's policy does in fact discriminate beyond disparate statistical data. Trends in recent decisions of the courts and their domination by the large number of Reagan appointees have liberals concerned about the future of civil rights remedies through the judicial process. Some observers have already expressed serious concerns over what they view as substantial reversals. Ralph Neas of the Leadership Conference on Civil Rights said, "More damage was done substantively to the civil rights laws in June 1989 than in the previous three-and-one half decades combined" (Moore, 1990, p. 1528). Many civil rights advocates were also gravely disappointed with President Bush's veto of the 1990 Civil Rights Act because it was what he described as a quota bill.

Affirmative action remains a highly controversial and extremely complex social and political issue. There is considerable disagreement among civil rights leaders and scholars themselves as to what governmental policies are best and even whether governmental action can provide solutions to the problems of discrimination. The Colby College historian Robert Weisbrot (1990) wrote: "Civil rights laws alone could not overcome the effects of past discrimination and lingering prejudice, nor did these laws substantially alter the economic system that had long permitted vast disparities of wealth and privilege to the disadvantage of most blacks." Some blacks feel that civil rights laws and policies such as affirmative action have in some ways been a mixed blessing. Shelby Steele, a black Professor of English at San Jose State University, holds that affirmative action has encouraged the discrimination it was supposed to end. Robert L. Woodson, president of the National Center for Neighborhood Enterprise, charged: "The interests of low-income blacks continue to be sacrificed on the altar of affirmative action. Civil rights remedies that call for statistical rather than economic parity are morally inconsistent, counter to the free enterprise system and [are] widening racial and economic gaps" (Moore, 1990, p. 1530). He and others call for programs and policies that will provide "economic empowerment" for blacks. William Julius Wilson, a black sociologist at the University of Chicago, has suggested that blacks should seriously consider abandoning policies designed specifically to benefit minorities only and push for new policies that are designed to overcome economic inequality for all segments of society. Wilson feels that although policies such as affirmative action have helped the black middle class, they have left the larger underclass virtually untouched. He also contends that many white Americans have turned against not so much blacks but policies and a strategy that have emphasized programs and approaches perceived to benefit only specific minorities. He concludes, therefore, that what are needed are programs and policies designed to expand employment opportunities and job skills training, improve education, provide adequate child and health care, and reduce neighborhood crime and drug abuse rather than race-specific measures (Wilson, 1987; see also DeParle. 1988; Jencks, 1988; Morely, 1988).

As Martin Luther King observed in the 1960s, it is one thing to integrate a lunch counter but quite another to be able to afford the lunch. The civil rights laws helped to open doors for blacks and other minorities; what they have not done—possibly can never do—is change traditional attitudes and behavior patterns. In spite of three decades of legislation, executive orders, and court decisions, discrimination remains a major social and economic problem. In the summer of 1990 the Urban Institute conducted studies in Chicago and Washington, D.C. Specially trained white and black college students with similar backgrounds and training responded to 476 randomly selected job advertisements. Despite their identical qualifications, whites advanced further 20% of the time; blacks 7% of the time. A similar study in 1989 showed even greater discrimination against Hispanic applicants. The institute concluded that discrimination was "widespread and entrenched" ("Job-seeking pairs find discrimination in hiring," 1991). With a growing economic underclass in our society demanding attention, many equal rights advocates are skeptical that a healthy dose of free enterprise capitalism holds the solution (DeParle, 1988; Wilson, 1987).

Sex Discrimination, Comparable Worth

The 1960s saw the civil rights movement in its height; the 1970s brought the women's movement. Books such as Betty Friedan's *The Feminine Mystique* (1963) and Kate Millett's *Sexual Politics* (1971) along with the founding of the National Organization for Women (NOW) in 1966 focused national attention on an array of women's issues. In the 1970s, along with affirmative action, gender moved to center stage as an employment issue. In the 1960s most job discrimination suits involved race; in the 1970s gender discrimination cases began coming to the court in growing numbers. In discrimination cases involving race, the Supreme Court had applied the doctrine of strict scrutiny, requiring that the challenged laws or policies be shown to serve a compelling public interest. For sex discrimination cases the majority opted for a more easily satisfied mid-level scrutiny, which required only there be a rational basis for laws or policies. In the 1973 case of *Frontiero v. Richardson* four justices argued for the strict scrutiny test, but the majority favored the mid-level approach. Nonetheless, they did strike down as sexually discriminatory a law that did not allow female service members to claim their spouses as dependents, saying that past paternalistic attitudes and actions had "put women not on a pedestal, but in a cage" (p. 684).

Though the majority on the Court agreed with Justice Lewis Powell, Jr., that discrimination based on sex was not "inherently odious," women were quite successful in using the courts to challenge sexually discriminatory laws and practices. In 1971 the Court struck down as sexually discriminatory a state law giving preference to men over women in administering an estate when the deceased had failed to name an administrator (*Reed v. Reed,* 1971). And in *Craig v. Boren* (1976), the Court ruled that gender-based distinctions are justified only if they serve some important governmental objective. Further, the courts have held that a compelling state interest allows treating women more favor-ably than men to compensate for the effects of past discrimination (*Kahn v. Shevin,* 1974). Since 1970 hundreds of suspect state and

Table 5.6 Females' Salaries Relative to Males' Salaries by Profession

For each $1,000 earned by males, females earn: Profession	*Female Earnings*
Lawyer	$878
Computer analyst	$780
Engineer	$828
Secretary/typist	$735
Information clerk	$726

SOURCE: From *The American Almanac of Jobs and Salaries* by John Wright and Edward Dwyer. Copyright © 1990 by John Wright and Edward Dwyer. Published by arrangement with Avon Books, a division of the Hearst Corporation. Reprinted with permission.

federal laws have been stricken as the courts have required gender distinctions to serve an "important government objective."

A major concern of the women's rights movement has been the inequity in pay received by male and female workers (see Tables 5.6, and 5.7). The Equal Pay Act passed in 1963 addressed only part of the problem in requiring equal pay for men and women performing the same work. Because persistent patterns of job segregation place many female workers in jobs staffed largely by women and because these jobs traditionally pay less than other jobs filled largely by males, women still experienced widespread pay inequity which the Equal Pay Act failed to address. As a consequence, the major women's issue of the 1980s became comparable worth, or pay equity. Those pushing this concept contend that pay should not be based on whether jobs are

Table 5.7 Comparative Salaries for Males and Females in Journalism

	Male	*Female*
Managing editor	$67,270	$43,691
Editorial page editor	57,767	42,750
City editor	45,142	39,055
Features editor	42,760	40,386
General reporter (longest tenure)	33,424	25,787

SOURCE: From *The American Almanac of Jobs and Salaries* by John Wright and Edward Dwyer. Copyright © 1990 by John Wright and Edward Dwyer. Published by arrangement with Avon Books, a division of the Hearst Corporation. Reprinted with permission.

largely male or female but on the value of the services provided to the employer by the employee. Under this concept, if the services provided by nurses, largely females, are of the same value as services provided by pharmacists, largely males, their salaries should be essentially the same because the jobs are of comparable worth to their employers.

Those pushing the comparable worth concept contend this is the only way the gap in pay between males and females can ever be closed. Opponents argue that comparable worth is an impossible concept to apply, maintaining that trying to determine the intrinsic value of different jobs is like comparing apples and oranges. Besides, they insist, the pay differential between men and women is a product of the job market and not something in which the government needs to be meddling. As more women move into jobs traditionally filled by men, this issue will take care of itself, they maintain. Proponents of pay equity reject such arguments, pointing out that when more women move into traditionally male jobs, it does not improve their salaries, but rather causes a decline in the salaries those jobs pay. Besides, point out the proponents, leaving this issue to job market forces will take forever to correct and this is an inequity that needs attention now. The comparable worth/pay equity movement was given a major boost with the 1981 decision in *County of Washington v. Gunther*. In this case female "matrons," who were paid $200 per month less than male "deputies," filed a sex discrimination suit; the Supreme Court found in their favor and upheld the concept of comparable worth. This marked the first time the courts had applied the concept in a pay discrimination suit.

Thus far the comparable worth movement has had more success at the state level. Twenty states have implemented plans providing pay equity adjustments for their employees and another 26 are reviewing pay policies. Overall the states have been quite responsive on the gender discrimination issue. Seventeen states now have provisions in their constitutions that prohibit discrimination based on gender. Several states have also enacted parental leave laws, and a number of others have such legislation under study. Progress has been made, but many issues remain and discrimination has not been eliminated from the workplace.

Conclusion

In a meeting in 1987 the nation's governors made welfare reform their top priority objective, recommending a shift in emphasis from income maintenance to work and training. The idea, not a new one, was that by stressing education and training, people would be prepared to gain jobs that paid enough to support their families. Although the idea is commendable, unaccompanied by comprehensive efforts to create more and better-paying jobs and to make the job market more equitable, it is almost surely doomed to fail.

Current trends in the U.S. economy and job market are not all that bright. From 1973 to 1984 about 20 million new jobs were added to the U.S. job market, but there was no growth in employment in the goods-producing sector. In fact, since 1981 the construction and manufacturing sectors have experienced a decline of over half a million jobs (Bluestone & Harrison, 1990). From 1979 to 1986 full-time employment grew about 14%, but for the same period growth in part-time employment was 50% greater. Almost 20% of the work force are part-time—about 19 million workers—and the median salary for part-time workers is only about 60% of that of full-time workers. Only about one third of part-time workers are covered by health insurance and only 20% are covered for pension benefits (Bluestone & Harrison, 1990). This growth in part-time workers is not a good sign for the economy.

Another problem is the trend toward lower paying jobs and growing income inequality. Barry Bluestone and Bennett Harrison (1990) cited a growing volume of research that all points in the same general direction—"a tendency toward low wages in particular and growing income inequality in general" (p. 619). They noted that from 1973 to 1978 approximately 12.1 million jobs were added to the work force and about two thirds of this increase was in jobs that paid $7,000 to $28,000. From 1979 to 1984 the U.S. work force grew by about 8 million new jobs, but well over one half of these new jobs paid less than $7,000 per year. During this period, higher paying jobs declined by over 5%. Certain groups will be particularly vulnerable to such trends. Between 1973 and 1986 the real median income for young people (aged 20-24) dropped by 27%; for young blacks the drop was almost 50%. More and more we find the nation facing a situation described by David R. Riemer (1988) in *The Prisoners of Welfare* as "not enough jobs and too many jobs that pay too little." Many metropolitan areas have experienced changing employment patterns that do not bode well for their economic future if new alternatives are not developed. In Louisville, Kentucky, for example, between 1975 and 1988 the metro area lost 26,000 manufacturing jobs. Those that were replaced were replaced by lower paying jobs, many of which were only part-time and provided few or no fringe benefits ("Sheltered forever," 1991). The Congressional

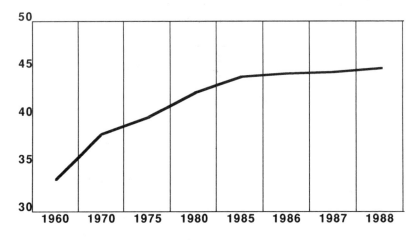

Figure 5.2. Females as Portion of Total Labor Force, 1960-1988
SOURCE: *Statistical Abstract of the United States*, 1990, p. 382.

Budget Office also reported that "within the industrial sector, the composition of employment has shifted toward lower paying jobs" (Clark 1987a, p. 399).

Current trends also make it even more imperative that inequities and discrimination be eliminated from the workplace. Presently about two thirds of all global immigration is to only one nation—the United States. The baby boom generation is already in the job market and the number of white, male job recruits is shrinking. In 1970 40% of the workforce was female; by 1990 the figure was over 50% and females were the fastest growing segment in the job market (see Figure 5.2). Estimates are that during the next decade well over one half of all job recruits will be females, minorities, and immigrants. Such prospects have already touched off a wide-ranging debate and changes in immigration laws. In 1990 Congress adopted changes increasing admission levels by 35%-40% to allow entry to more foreign workers and their families. The changes touched off concerns about the interrelationship of immigration and the employment prospects of Americans, especially those at the bottom of the economic ladder. Is the more appropriate policy the importing of workers or the training of our own unskilled indigenous population? Congressman John Bryant (D., TX) said: "I think it is really

Table 5.8 Numbers of EEOC Complaints and Suits

	1981	*1986*	*1990*
Complaints filed	53,700	65,666	62,135
Suits filed	368	410	501
Suits resolved	237	386	546

an unfortunate concept to say we have to import labor into this country when we have an unemployment rate in excess of 5.5 percent" (Kirschten, 1990a, p. 537). In an approach most of his colleagues found too novel, Congressman Bruce Morrison (D., CT) proposed a tax on employers hiring foreign workers to be used to fund training programs for un-skilled and unemployed Americans (Kirschten, 1990b, p. 537). Many question whether immigration holds the solution to U.S. economic and employment problems. They agree with Robert Bach and Doris Meiss-ner of the Carnegie Endowment for International Peace's Immigration Policy Project who concluded that immigration was not the solution because the labor shortages are not so much in numbers as in skills ("Infofile: Immigration," 1990). Importing workers can pose other problems as well, as has been demonstrated by sanctions in the 1986 Immigration Reform and Control Act against employers who hire ille-gal aliens. According to some studies, the unintended effect of this provision has been employer discrimination against foreign-born citi-zens and legal aliens for fear of violating the law (Kirschten, 1990b).

Changing patterns of U.S. population make discrimination in em-ployment an even greater concern in the country's economic future. In 1980 only 6% of the U.S. population was born abroad, but liberalized immigration laws and a heavy rate of illegal immigration in the 1980s have increased this proportion. Also, within the United States, growth in the population has been fastest among nonwhite groups. From 1980 to 1988 white population grew by only 6%, whereas the black popula-tion grew by 13% and the Hispanic by 34% (Wilson, 1990b). These trends mean that more and more prospective workers are going to be minority, and if our nation is to realize their full potential, the employ-ment patterns of the Reagan years will have to undergo some changes.

Civil rights and equal opportunity were low priority during Reagan's two terms, with emphasis on voluntary compliance. Though complaints to the EEOC actually increased, the number of suits filed declined (see

Table 5.8). By 1983 the number of suits filed by the EEOC had dropped 60% from the 1980 level. The same was true for the Office of Federal Contract Compliance Programs (OFCCP), as complaints filed against contractors dropped from 53 in FY 1980 to only 5 in FY 1982 and 19 in FY 1983. The amount of back pay awarded to those discriminated against dropped from $9 million in FY 1980 to under $4 million for FY 1983. The budgets and staffs of both agencies were also reduced under Reagan; the EEOC by 10 and 12%, respectively, and the OFCCP by 24 and 34%, respectively. The Civil Rights Division of the Justice Department also suffered a 13% reduction in staff. Probably even more significant, however, was the change in philosophy from relying on evidence of discriminatory effect to requiring proof of intent to discriminate. And along with this shift in emphasis came the attitude that the consequences of past discrimination have to be corrected only when individual victims can be identified. These shifts have resulted in a major change in the definition of the federal government's role and responsibility for the enforcement of civil rights and equal opportunity. President Bush has continued in this vein, vetoing the 1990 Civil Rights Act saying it was a quota bill. Congress came close, but fell just short of mustering enough votes to override the veto.

The Reagan years reflect a backlash against the more vigorous enforcement policies of earlier administrations and the activism of the civil rights and feminist groups. Such attitudes run counter to what is needed to respond effectively to the growing problems of poverty, homelessness, joblessness, and income inequality in our society. Efforts to advance social, political, and economic equality are always controversial and divisive; but in a highly pluralistic, democratic system such as ours, the continuing struggle for the advancement of these goals is the glue that holds the system together. Should numbers of citizens ever decide that the attainment of equality and fairness have ceased to be goals of the system, then its foundation is in danger. Furthermore, from a more practical economic standpoint, ensuring broader opportunity and greater equity for all citizens may be the only really viable means of achieving the more productive and competitive economy necessary for survival in the global marketplace.

Note

1. In the first case to come before it involving the Fourteenth Amendment, the *Slaughterhouse Cases* of 1873, the U.S. Supreme Court ruled that impairment of property rights by statute violated the due process clause. In subsequent cases the Court inserted freedom of contracts into the due process clause and a variety of state and federal regulatory efforts were held invalid as a consequence. In *Hammer v. Dagenhart* (1918) and again in *Bailey v. Drexel Furniture Co.* (1922) the Court disallowed congressional efforts to regulate child labor, and in *Adkins v. Children's Hospital* (1923) it struck down a wages and hours law. Finally in the late 1930s the Court began to move away from interpreting freedom of contract and due process as prohibiting governmental regulation. In *West Coast Hotel Co. v. Parrish* (1937), the Court overruled *Adkins* and upheld Washington state's minimum wage law, and in *U.S. v. Darby* (1941) the Court upheld the Fair Labor Standards Act, which established wages and hours for workers producing goods for interstate commerce and placed restrictions on the use of child labor.

6

Helping Children and Families

Since the 1930s one of the major growth areas in federal policy has been in the realm of family programs as more and more family-related issues have been brought into the political arena. Covering a broad spectrum of public efforts, family and child welfare policies are closely interwoven with several other policy sectors such as health, nutrition, education, and income maintenance, making them a somewhat confusing patchwork of policies and programs.

Background

Traditionally the family has been perceived as a central and essential institution in U.S. society, performing many functions crucial to the social, political, and economic systems. Of growing concern to many has been the decline of the traditional family in modern U.S. society and consequently the decline in the family's role in performing many of its traditional functions. The extended family of generations past has become much less common today with only a few modern-day households containing members of more than one adult generation. Likewise the traditional family pattern of two parents—a wage-earning father and a homemaker mother—is much less common today. A study by the Ford

Table 6.1 Distribution of Families by Type, 1960-1988

Type of Family	1960	1970	1975	1980	1985	1987	1988	1990
All Families (millions)								
Married couple	24.1	26.1	25.9	25.6	25.0	25.6	25.5	24.5
Single parent								
Female	2.5	3.4	4.9	6.0	6.8	7.1	7.2	8.4
Male	0.3	0.4	0.5	0.7	1.1	1.1	1.3	1.3
White Families (%)								
Married couple				83.7	81.0	80.4	80.6	
Single parent								
Female				14.2	15.8	16.3	16.1	
Male				2.1	3.2	3.3	3.6	
Hispanic Families (%)								
Married couple	NA	NA	77.8	75.3	71.7	70.8	69.8	
Single parent								
Female	NA	NA	18.7	20.1	23.0	23.4	23.4	
Male	NA	NA	3.5	4.6	5.3	5.8	6.8	
Black Families (%)								
Married couple	NA	NA	55.9	48.8	44.3	46.5	45.4	
Single parent								
Female	NA	NA	55.9	48.8	44.3	46.5	45.4	
Male	NA	NA	2.7	3.2	3.9	3.9	4.5	

SOURCE: U.S. Bureau of the Census (1990, p. 21).

Foundation (1989c) reported in 1989 that only one in ten U.S. families (10%) fit the traditional concept (see Table 6.1). As nontraditional families become more and more common, there is virtually no consensus on exactly what a "family" is. A variety of factors have contributed to this decline and confusion.

Single-Parent Families

Recent decades have brought a dramatic increase in the number of single-parent families as both divorce rates and out-of-wedlock births have grown (see Figure 6.1 and Table 6.2). The Census Bureau reported 9.7 million single parents in 1990, a 41% increase over 1980. The number of single parents grew 82% since 1970. About 87% of single parents are female ("Decline in 'married-with-children' lifestyle slowed in U.S. during '80s," 1991). Since 1970 the number of children with divorced parents has doubled and the number with a never-wed parent

Millions

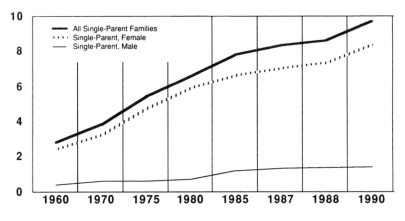

Figure 6.1. Growth in Single-Parent Families, 1960-1990

grew sixfold. From 1970 to 1987 the number of divorces in the United States grew from 708,000 to 1,163,000 (*World Almanac,* 1990, p. 839). At present rates, two of every five white youngsters and three of every five black youngsters will experience divorce, not once, but twice in their lifetime. As many as 75% of black children born to a married mother may experience divorce in the family before reaching age 16 (U.S. Congress, House Select Committee on Children, Youth and Families, 1989). From 1960 to 1979 out-of-wedlock births among teenagers tripled. In 1950 only 4% of all births were to unwed mothers as compared to 25% of all babies born in 1988. The 1988 figure marked an 8% jump over 1987 and a 50% increase over 1980 ("Births among unmarried women concern researchers," 1991). Of major concern was the number of births to unwed teenagers, as such mothers were much more likely to be impoverished and end up on welfare. In 1970, 50% of all unwed births were to teenagers, but by 1986 this figure was down to 33% as two out of three births to unmarried females that year were to women over the age of 20. A continuing cause for concern is that the proportion of births to teenage mothers that occur outside of marriage continues to grow (U.S. Congress, House Select Committee on Children, Youth and Families, 1989, p. ix). Due to divorce and births to unwed mothers, many of whom are only teenagers, more and more

Table 6.2 Marriage and Divorce Rates, 1900-1989

| | Marriages | | Divorces/Annulments | |
Year	Number (thousands)	Rate (per thousand)	Number (thousands)	Rate (per thousand)
1900	709	9.3	56	0.7
1910	948	10.3	104	1.0
1920	1,274	12.0	171	1.6
1930	1,126	9.2	196	1.6
1940	1,595	12.1	264	2.0
1950	1,667	11.1	385	2.6
1960	1,523	8.5	393	2.2
1965	1,800	9.3	479	2.5
1970	2,159	10.6	709	3.5
1975	2,153	10.0	1,036	4.8
1980	2,390	10.6	1,189	5.2
1982	2,456	10.6	1,170	5.0
1984	2,477	10.5	1,169	5.0
1986	2,407	10.0	1,178	4.9
1989	2,404	9.7	1,163	4.7
	% Increase 1900-1989 239	% Increase 1900-1989 4.3	% Increase 1900-1989 1,977	% Increase 1900-1989 571

SOURCES: U.S. Bureau of the Census (1991, p. 86); *World Almanac* (1990, p. 839).

households have become single-parent households. From 1970 to 1990 the proportion of households composed of married couples with children living at home declined from 40% to less than 30%. Put another way, over 25% of U.S. families with children at home are headed by a single parent, and the Ford Foundation (1989c) projects that more than one half the children born in the United States today will live in a single-parent family before reaching age 18. In 1990 over one half of all black families with children were single-parent whereas about 30% of Hispanic families and about one fifth of all white families with children fell into that category. Ninety percent of one-parent families are headed by single mothers. Between 1980 and 1988 the number of children living with their mothers only grew from 11.4 million to 13.5 million, a 21% increase (U.S. Congress, House Select Committee on Children, Youth and Families, 1989).

This high incidence of single-parent households headed by women is a factor contributing to the high poverty rates among children. About

Table 6.3 Percent of Children Under 18 Living in Families Below Poverty Level

Year	All Families	White Families	Black Families	Female-Headed Families
1979	16.0	11.4	40.8	48.6
1984	21.0	16.1	46.2	54.0
1985	20.1	15.6	43.1	53.6
1986	19.8	15.3	42.7	54.4
1987	20.0	15.0	45.1	54.7

SOURCE: U.S. Bureau of the Census (1990, p. 459).

one fifth of all children in the United States now live in poverty; for minorities the figure is 40%-50%; and in 1987 almost 55% of children who lived in female-headed households were poor. Children who live in single-parent, female-headed households are two and one half times as likely to be poor as those in two-parent families. Female-headed families have a 34% poverty rate whereas for two-parent families the rate is 6%. Black and Hispanic female-headed families have an even higher poverty rate of over 50%. Black children living in single-parent, female-headed families have a 56% poverty rate whereas for white children in a similar setting the rate is 19%. For black youngsters living with their mothers only, 91% are poor (Bawden & Palmer, 1982; Brazelton, 1991; "Children of poverty," 1989; Fulton, 1986; U.S. Congress, House Select Committee on Children, Youth and Families, 1989; see Table 6.3).

A factor contributing to the financial plight of the single-parent, female-headed family is the fact that many of the absent fathers pay little or no child support. A family split usually has a dramatically different effect economically for the male and female: Males most often experience an increase in their standard of living, whereas females experience an even sharper decline in theirs. Almost 9 million women have children under 21 living with them whose fathers are absent. About 40% were never awarded child support and about half those who were received less than the full amount due, many of them none at all. The House Select Committee on Children, Youth and Families (1989) reported these findings: 24% received no support, 25.5% received less than was awarded, 50.5% received the full amount, and 42% were awarded no support. The Department of Health and Human Services estimates that unpaid child support amounts to over $3 billion annually. Consequently, about one third of those families where the father is absent live in poverty (Kosterlitz, 1987a).

On the assumption that improved collections of child support payments could reduce welfare costs, enable some families to get off the welfare rolls, and reduce the poverty rate among children, Congress in 1974 passed legislation putting in place the Child Support Enforcement Program (CSE) and in 1984 tightened the provisions further. Under this program the federal government provides funding to the states to encourage more vigorous collection of child support payments. For those on AFDC the state collects the child support owed and if the family leaves AFDC the support payments revert back to the family. Funds are also provided to improve the collection rates for families not on AFDC. Although some see these reforms as a step toward reducing the single-parent family's dependency on AFDC and often impoverished condition, others remain skeptical of the effort's success. Thus far the states have not been all that enthusiastic in helping to enforce these provisions because they don't benefit all that much. Others see the reforms as benefiting women not on welfare more than those who are because the husbands of mothers who are on welfare will be the ones least likely and least able to pay. The skeptics point out that upper-income white fathers are the ones owing the most child support whereas black children are the ones most in need. Therefore, improved collection levels may not provide the funds where they are needed most.

Since the 1970s families with children have fared worse economically than other families. As productivity and economic growth slowed from 1970 to 1990, the inequality for families with children grew at a higher rate than for families without children. Two factors in particular probably help explain this. Younger people more likely to have children at home experienced greater economic stress as is shown in these figures: In 1956 28.5% of younger people had high incomes, 42.6% had median incomes, and 28.8% were in the low-income category; but by 1986 only 25.2% had high incomes, 29.6% had median incomes, and 45.2% were now in the low-income group. In 1973 the average annual income for a head of family under 30 years of age was $19,243; by 1986 that figure was $13,500. Among low-income families with children, average family income declined 14% between 1979 and 1987 even as that of the highest-income families grew by 19%. The younger the family, the worse they fared economically during the 1970s and 1980s ("Births among unmarried women concern researchers," 1991; U.S.

Table 6.4 Distribution of Incomes by Families, 1988

Income Levels	All Families	White Families	Black Families	Hispanic Families
Median Income (dollars)	32,191	33,915	19,329	21,769
Income Under $5,000 (%)	4.0	3.0	11.9	8.4
$15,000-$24,999 (%)	17.8	17.7	19.7	8.4
$25,000-$34,999 (%)	16.9	17.4	13.4	15.5
$35,000-$49,999 (%)	20.0	21.0	13.3	11.9
$50,000 + (%)	25.7	27.4	12.6	11.9

SOURCE: U.S. Bureau of the Census (1991, pp. 450-451).

Congress, House Select Committee on Children, Youth and Families, 1989, pp. x-xi; Table 6.4). Over the same period the number of single-parent families almost doubled, and as their numbers have grown their income has fallen. From 1973 to 1984 the average real earnings for younger males (aged 20-24) fell about 30% (50% for blacks); at the same time marriage rates dropped and the number of out-of-wedlock births soared. Pregnancy rates among unwed teenage girls jumped 20% since 1970, and two thirds of these teenage mothers spend some time in poverty. The average number of years in poverty for single mothers is 7; for a black mother, 12 (Cochran, 1990).

Marvin Kosters of the American Enterprise Institute (AEI), a conservative think tank, said, "I think we have a terrible problem of too many children being raised in family situations where incomes are low" (Rauch, 1989, p. 2042). About 13 million children were estimated to be living in households with incomes below the poverty level in 1988, and the Congressional Budget Office estimated there are almost 3 million youngsters below age 6 living in female-headed households that are below the poverty level (Dobelstein, 1990). Poverty becomes more and more a problem faced by children and women. From 1960 to 1988 the proportion of families headed by females grew from 10% to 28% and the proportion of the population living below the poverty line that was in such households doubled. If current trends continue, by the year 2000 almost all U.S. poor may be in female-headed households—elderly widows and single mothers. This is the increasing "feminization"of poverty.

Poverty can have particularly severe consequences for infants and children. In 1988 the United States had an infant mortality rate of 9.9

per 1,000 live births and for 1989 the figure was only slightly better at 9.7. This rate has not declined significantly from 1980 to 1990 and is higher than the rate for most other industrialized countries. Among black babies the rate is almost double at 17.9 per 1,000 live births. A factor contributing to the poor ranking of the United States may well be the numbers of babies born to teenage mothers and mothers living in poverty. A disproportionately high percentage of infants born to mothers without the financial and other resources to care for them properly tend to have low birth weights and other health problems. Low birth weight is seen as the primary cause for this high infant mortality rate and many see this as poverty related. One study estimated that as many as one fourth of infants who die could be saved by adequate prenatal care for high-risk mothers ("At a glance," 1990). The national Commission to Prevent Infant Mortality claims that 57%-65% of low-birth-weight babies are born to mothers who simply do not eat properly. In addition to the high mortality rate, the Office of Technology Assessment estimated in a 1988 study that each low-birth-weight baby cost the taxpayers $14,000 to $30,000 in health care expenses (Wilson, 1990b). Conservatives dispute such claims, contending that low birth weights are more a result of ethnic, genetic, and other factors than diet. Various studies have also shown that children from poor families tend to lag significantly in developmental skills and frequently require more intensive and more specialized services to correct their problems. Children from single-parent, female-headed households are more likely to demonstrate antisocial behavioral tendencies and poor school performance. Children from poor families have higher school dropout rates, miring them even deeper into the poverty cycle (Dobelstein, 1990).

Working Mothers

Another major change in the U.S. family pattern has been the significant increase in the number of mothers who work outside the home (see Table 6.5); in 1950 only 22% of mothers with children under 18 worked outside the home, but by 1990 that figure was approaching 60%. In 1970 only about 40% of the work force was female; by 1991 almost 50% of all workers were female, and this number will increase before the end of the century. In 1950 only 12% of mothers with at least one child under 6 years of age worked. By 1987, 57% of these mothers were working. By the 1990s, 12 million youngsters under 6 years of age had mothers working outside the home, as 70% of U.S. women aged 25-44 were in

Table 6.5 Percentage of Mothers With Children Who Work Outside the Home,
1970-1988

Age of Children	1970	1975	1980	1985	1986	1987	1988
0-5 yrs.	29	36	43	49	50	53	77
6-17 yrs.	43	47	57	62	62	64	50
under 18 yrs.	39	44	53	58	58	60	54

SOURCE: U.S. Department of Labor, Bureau of Labor Statistics, Bulletin No. 87-345, p. 77.

the paid work force. The National Research Council estimated that by the year 2000, 80% of school-aged youngsters and 70% of preschoolers will have mothers working outside the home ("Infofile," 1990b; U.S. Congress, House Select Committee on Children, Youth and Families, 1989). Many working mothers held two jobs; in the 1980s the number of women working two jobs more than doubled. The Congressional Budget Office estimated that from 1980 to 1990 the number of children with two parents and a working mother grew 36% whereas the number with two parents and a mother not working dropped 10% (U.S. Congress, House Select Committee on Children, Youth and Families, 1989). These trends produced growing concerns about "latchkey" kids and focused more attention on such issues as child care and parental leave.

Major Issues

Debates over child and family assistance programs produce all the usual issues concerning social welfare policies. When the federal government does choose to address such issues, and it usually does so reluctantly, it is viewed by some as intruding upon the prerogatives of both the family and other levels of government. Consequently, many efforts in this area are joint federal-state programs.

As a noncontributory program, AFDC in particular comes in for considerable criticism. Because until just recently, it provided aid to children in families only when the father was absent, there was some concern in the 1960s and 1970s that AFDC was contributing to "family breakup." Conservative critics charged that the program encouraged fathers in poor families to leave home so the family could qualify for benefits. The program now includes families in which both parents are in the home but the major breadwinner is unemployed. This change should alleviate the family breakup issue.

AFDC has also been criticized for being a disincentive to work and for contributing to welfare dependency. Conservative critics charge that many able-bodied females prefer to stay home with their children and draw benefits under the program rather than seek gainful employment. They also contend that children growing up in such a setting are more likely to end up on welfare, thus creating a welfare class in society. In 1991, the newly elected conservative governor of California, Pete Wilson (R.), proposed to reduce welfare spending 9%. At that time California's benefits under AFDC were second only to Alaska's, and Wilson proposed reductions in benefits to 2.1 million recipients, mostly single mothers. When proposing the cuts, Wilson said recipients might "have less for a six-pack of beer" but would not really be hurt. The existing program, he contended, "risks perpetuating dependency from generation to generation" (Kosterlitz, 1988a; Wagman, 1991). Liberal defenders of the program challenge the validity of such charges, pointing out that most beneficiaries stay on the program for less than 2 years, using it to temporarily support them through financial difficulties. They maintain that although some families do stay on AFDC for extended periods—10 years or longer—there is little hard evidence that even they would rather be on welfare than gainfully employed (Chisman & Pifer, 1987; Dobelstein, 1990; Morris & Williamson, 1986; Schwartz, 1988; Wagman, 1991). In fact, they point to evidence that would tend to refute such claims. In 1981 the Reagan administration changed the AFDC regulations to substantially reduce the amounts mothers could earn without reducing their benefits and at the same time made about half a million women ineligible to continue drawing benefits. Almost none of the mothers whose benefits were reduced quit working as a result (Chisman & Pifer, 1987). One third of all families below the poverty level have at least one member of the family working full-time (Dobelstein, 1990). More on disincentives later.

Another charge was that AFDC tended to encourage illegitimacy by subsidizing unwed mothers to have more children. Because a mother could increase her benefits by having more children, some contended that a limit should be placed on the number of dependents per family. The patterns of change in illegitimate births tend to discredit this argument. As AFDC benefits have been reduced, illegitimate birth rates have continued to grow. Most research shows no positive relationship between level of benefits and the rate of illegitimate births (Chisman &

Pifer, 1987). But many continue to use this as an argument against the program. Reflecting this sentiment to some degree, Wisconsin Governor Tommy Thompson (R.) proposed that his state impose a ceiling on benefits to unwed mothers who continued to bear children even as teenage mothers who married would become entitled to larger payments. In proposing a pilot program for four counties, the governor assumed that marriage is a key to curbing welfare dependency. Supporters of this approach see family breakdown and the poverty cycle as going hand in hand and point out that a family with both husband and wife in the home is 30% less likely to be poor than a family headed by an unwed mother. According to those supporting this concept, an intact family with at least one parent working has a better than 95% chance of staying above the poverty level ("Helping teenage mothers who marry is plan's goal," 1991). In Massachusetts, the conservative Democratic candidate for governor John R. Silber proposed abolishing welfare for unwed teenage mothers who bore a second child. He lost his 1990 bid for the governorship.

Efforts at Solution

Programs aimed at protecting children are among the oldest social programs in the United States. Children themselves, of course, cannot vote and are not politically active, but their cause has been pushed by various groups for decades. The New York Children's Aid Society was founded in 1853 and was joined in the cause of child protection by the New York Society for the Prevention of Cruelty to Children in 1870. In 1909 President Theodore Roosevelt convened the first White House Conference on Children and in 1912 the Children's Bureau was established in the Department of Labor. It is now a division of the Department of Health and Human Services (HHS).

By 1900 half of the states had adopted laws regulating the use of child labor, and starting with Illinois in 1911 the states began to adopt programs providing financial support for dependent children in their own homes. Prior to these programs, the common practice had been to remove children from families financially unable to care for them properly, an approach no longer supported under modern welfare concepts. Congress also passed federal child labor laws in the early part of the 1900s, but these early efforts were held unconstitutional by the Supreme Court. Such provisions were eventually made a part of the Fair

Labor Standards Act of 1938 (see Chapter 5). The Sheppard-Towner Act of 1921 created a federal program in maternal and child health to provide assistance to mothers and newborn babies.

By the 1930s several states had programs that provided assistance to widows and their children. The federal Social Security Act of 1935 provided for grants to the states for a variety of services and support for mothers and children. These block grants can be used by the states for maternal and child health services, services to handicapped children, and general child welfare programs. They cover such items as care for mothers prior to and after childbirth, immunization of children against communicable diseases, therapy and rehabilitation for handicapped children whose parents lack the means for appropriate care, and child welfare services such as counseling and care for neglected children, mentally retarded or emotionally disturbed youngsters, and delinquents. Altogether the Social Security Act contains eight titles that either directly or indirectly provide services benefiting children, including:

Title II Retirement and Disability Insurance—Covers children under age 18 if their parents are covered.

Title III Unemployment Insurance—Provides family income support for covered parents when out of work.

Title IV Aid to Families With Dependent Children (AFDC)—More on this later.

Title V Maternal and Child Health Programs.

Title XVI Supplemental Security Income—Income maintenance for those not covered by other programs.

Title XIX Medicaid—Provides medical services for children in families of welfare recipients.

Because the states already had programs supporting maternal and child services, the federal program was intended to supplement and expand these available services. Because these programs are state administered, the individual states retain considerable discretion in determining eligibility standards and benefit levels. Therefore, these programs may vary substantially state to state.

Aid to Families With Dependent Children

The largest, most costly, and most controversial of these social assistance programs is AFDC. With roots in the state programs for assisting widows and their dependent children, this program is designed to provide both income maintenance and social services. A means-tested program, AFDC provides monthly benefits to dependent children and their adult caretaker(s), usually their mothers. Although eligibility requirements vary state to state, as a general rule the mother or caretaker must have dependent children and no other means of support. Income usually cannot exceed $3,000 and the recipient can have few other personal assets. The typical AFDC recipient is a white woman working full- or part-time in a low-paying job.

From its inception, the program has been plagued by contradictions in its goals and administration and the object of continuing controversy. The program was not designed as a cure for poverty or a work incentive program; its sole purpose was to protect the children of poor families by supplementing their income. It was planned as a limited and tempo-rary income maintenance program. For several years benefits were restricted to mothers of children in homes where no male breadwinner was present. But as traditional family patterns changed, with more mothers working, divorces becoming more frequent, and out-of-wedlock births soaring, pressures to broaden coverage grew. In 1967 the rules were changed to extend benefits to single mothers and subsequently to families where the father was in the home but out of work. Only about one half the states have implemented these changes, however. Despite this hesitancy on the part of the states, growth in the numbers of single mothers and children with living fathers who did not support them financially caused the number of families on AFDC to double between 1962 and 1970. Most of these new recipients were young mothers or mothers who had their first child while still a teenager. Women who were teenagers when they gave birth to their first child, whether married or not, receive more than half the benefits paid under AFDC. New applicants usually seek benefits because of the departure of a husband or the birth of a child out of wedlock (Bawden & Palmer, 1982).

Because conservative critics charge AFDC with fostering welfare dependency and many view its recipients as loafers and chiselers, the program has been changed in various efforts to strengthen the ties between work and the receipt of benefits. Under 1960 changes, mothers who had no preschool children were required to work to receive bene-fits. Other rules, however, tended to counter this objective. Prior to 1967, an AFDC recipient who worked forfeited $1 in benefits for each $1 earned. This rule was modified in 1967 to provide that the first $30 of income each month was disregarded altogether and benefit levels were calculated on one third of the remaining monthly income. In 1981 the Reagan administration modified this regulation, resulting in a reduction in benefits for about 300,000 families with a working member and making about 400,000 families ineligible for the program altogether. So the government appears to be sending mixed signals on the work incentive issue. If you do not work, you are ineligible; if you do work, you lose part or all of your benefits.

With welfare programs, and AFDC in particular, under widespread attack, President Nixon told a national television audience on August 8, 1969, "It [welfare assistance] breaks up homes. It often penalizes work. It robs recipients of dignity. And it grows" (Nixon, 1971). To reform the system he proposed the Family Assistance Plan (FAP), saying it "would create a much stronger incentive to work." The FAP would have provided a minimum benefit nationwide under AFDC and for the first time would have provided benefits to about 28 million "working poor." But Nixon was unable to sell his "guaranteed income" plan to either liberals or conservatives. The former considered the proposed cash payments of $1,600 to $2,200 as far too stingy, and the latter as too generous. The National Welfare Rights Organization called for a payment of at least $5,500 for a family of four (*Congress and the Nation,* 1973).

The debate over how to reduce "welfare dependency" continued into the Carter administration. In 1977 President Carter unveiled his proposal for welfare reform in the Program for Better Jobs and Income. He proposed to drop the AFDC, SSI, and food stamp programs and replace them with cash payments to about 32 million persons, including the working poor. His plan would have included the creation of up to 1.4 million public service jobs to help employ those receiving benefits under the program. Carter's proposal also failed to gain the necessary support in Congress.

The push for welfare reform continued as the nation's governors made it their top priority in 1987. They called for a shift from income maintenance to more emphasis on work and training, with AFDC being changed to an income support approach tied to work. Finally on the third attempt since the mid-1960s, AFDC was revamped under the Family Support Act approved by Congress in 1988. This act strengthened the child support enforcement procedures in an effort to collect more of the child support owed by delinquent fathers; required the states to implement work, education, and training programs for welfare mothers; required the states to extend benefits to poor two-parent families when the primary wage earner is unemployed; and called for transitional services for families when welfare parents go to work, including medical coverage and child care benefits for up to a year. The hallmark of the reforms was the Job Opportunities and Basic Skills Training (JOBS) program, which required all able-bodied adults in AFDC households to work or participate in job training or education to receive benefits.

These reforms addressed some of the problems of the family assistance programs, but they still were inadequate in many respects. To date efforts to tie welfare benefits to job training and work have not proven very successful. Obstacles to the success of such programs are numerous and quite complex, not the least being the often contradictory policies and expectations of the government itself. Together with initiatives such as the Work Incentives Program (WIN) and JOBS, the federal and state administering agencies adopted other policies and regulations that made it difficult or impossible for people to leave welfare even if they found work. A 1986 study in Wisconsin showed that if a single mother who had two children went to work and raised her earnings from $3,350 to $5,025 she had to give up 80% of her additional earnings under the existing guidelines. For her efforts she got to keep $335 of her earnings even as she gave up $1,340. Yet another case study revealed that a mother who went from a part-time job paying $5,000 to a full-time job paying about $10,000 ended up $150 ahead after losing her AFDC payment and paying for child care so she could work. She also, of course, lost her medicaid benefits. How do you encourage persons on welfare to seek gainful employment when they encounter an effective marginal tax rate of 75% to 95%? President Bush and many in Congress thought 33% was a disincentive for those earning $200,000 or more a year.

The 1988 reforms have only partially addressed this issue by providing certain transitional services for up to a year, including coverage under medicaid. Another obstacle also addressed by this act was that of child care. In 1990 about 65% of women who were working had children at home, and for poor women in particular adequate child care was a major concern. AFDC mothers who work are allowed to deduct up to $160 per month per child from their gross earnings for costs of child care in determining their level of AFDC benefits. This, however, constitutes only a partial subsidy for the actual cost to most. The 1988 JOBS program guaranteed day care assistance for mothers who were required under its provisions to work. The bigger problem, however, was finding available facilities. At the start of the 1990s public support programs paid only for care in state-licensed facilities. This posed two major problems. First, there were not enough of these facilities available. At that time public-funded day care served only about 10% of the children in poor families. Second, most of the working poor arranged for the care of their children through relatives or friends. The provisions of 1988 did not allow for this alternative. According to a 1989 study by the Children's Defense Fund, 48% of child care was provided by relatives, 22% by family day care homes, 23% by child care or preschool centers, and 6% by nonrelatives in the child's home ("The numbers game," 1990).

Because child care is such a vital issue to working mothers and a key to the success of jobs programs for those on welfare, it continues to be an issue for discussion in Congress. In the 1980-1988 sessions of Congress almost 60 different child care bills have been introduced. In 1988 Congress considered the Act for Better Child Care Services (the ABC bill), but could not come to a final agreement. President Bush outlined a $2.5 billion package that would provide a tax credit of up to $1,000 per child under 4 years of age to low-income parents, expand tax credits for dependent care, provide support to private employers who provide child care facilities, and expand funding for the Head Start Program. His proposals met a mixed response in Congress.

Throughout the 1980s and into the 1990s pressures continued to grow for some governmental action on the child care and parental leave issues. These changed from primarily union issues to items of general concern. In 1989 the president and Congress appointed the 36-member National Commission on Children to study and report on the status of the next generation of Americans. A host of other groups and foundations joined the commission in looking at various aspects of the status of the nation's children. In June 1990 the U.S. Advisory Board on Child Abuse and Neglect declared a "child protection emergency" (Kosterlitz, 1990c, p. 2120). A joint report of the Center for the Study of Social Policy and the Annie E. Casey Foundation termed the 1980s "a terrible decade for children"; the report noted that the rate for jailing children during the decade grew by 41%, the poverty rate among those under 18 grew from 16% in 1979 to 20.1% in 1989, the proportion of unmarried teens giving birth rose from 7.5% in 1980 to 8.2% in 1988, and the rate of violent death among those under 18 rose by 12% ("1980s called 'terrible decade' for children in U.S."). Yet another study by the National Institute of Justice reported that abused or neglected children were more likely to become involved in crime, suffer academically and socially, and turn to drugs or alcohol ("The perils of abuse," 1991). The Howard University sociologist Joyce A. Ladner noted, "We're seeing increasing numbers of children who are not getting adequate care and for whom adequate care is not an imminent possibility" (Kosterlitz, 1990c, p. 2120).

Although support for child and parental leave programs continued to grow, neither President Bush nor Congress came forward with a comprehensive plan. In 1990 Congress passed a family leave measure that provided up to 12 weeks of unpaid annual leave to parents of a newborn or newly adopted child or to those with a family member who was seriously ill. The measure was vetoed by President Bush and the House sustained the veto by 53 votes, with 57 Democrats supporting the president against the override attempt. A similar measure was reintroduced in the 102nd Congress, but some view this measure not so much a "profamily" matter as an "antibusiness" measure. Despite the widening appeal of such programs, many political leaders still feel that family programs like child care and family leave pay quite meager political dividends. In 1990 only about one household in three had a small child at home and parents with young children are only half as likely to vote as are parents with grown children. Likewise the poor are only half as likely to vote as the rich (Taylor, 1991). Jean Mayer, president of Tufts University, claimed, "Americans in general are not much interested in children" (*National Journal,* February 17, 1990, p. 389). Congressman Charles Stenholm (D., TX) summed up a major concern shared by many of his colleagues when he observed: "You can benefit people, but they don't remember it very long. But they remember that tax bill" (*National Journal,* June 2, 1990, p. 1337). Such perceptions make getting the necessary votes difficult. Action was further complicated in the 101st Congress when the family bills got caught up in an internal power struggle between two House committees. The Human Resources subcommittee of the powerful Ways and Means committee chaired by Congressman Thomas Downey (D., NY) was pushing its own measure and the House Education and Labor committee was championing another version. With this turf battle pulling committee members in all directions, action was blocked for the session. New measures were under consideration in the 102nd Congress.

During the 1970s and 1980s, conservative elements dominated the discussions on family issues and they tended to brand the government as the problem, not the route to solution. Such problems, they maintained, could be better solved through market solutions. At the start of the 1990s liberals began to take up the cause for such programs again, as was foreshadowed in New York Governor Mario Cuomo's address to the Democratic Convention in 1988. As they assume the mantle for such causes again, the liberals are seeking to redirect the issue from its moral and cultural overtones to one primarily of economics. Regardless of the basis on which these issues are approached, many proponents see expanded child care and leave policies as essential to any successful effort at overall welfare reform. They maintain there is a positive correlation between low income and poor child care and that children from families in poverty can benefit greatly from adequate day care. Not only does the lack of adequate child care aggravate the plight of children in poor households, contend the proponents, it is a major factor keeping welfare mothers from working. Denise Polit and Joseph O'Hara (1989) found child care to be the most critical service needed by single mothers if they were to achieve self-sufficiency, and the House Select Committee on Children, Youth and Families (1989) found more economically disadvantaged mothers would seek work if they could find affordable child care.

Many questions remain to be resolved. Should child care programs aid all families with children or just those with incomes below a certain level? Should subsidies for child care go to parents and guardians or to the providers of services? Or to both? Should subsidies be direct cash benefits, vouchers, or tax credits? These are only a few of the often complex questions raised by this issue. Some fear that if such issues are not resolved soon, current policies could lead to a two-tier system of child care that would contribute to the already widening gap between low-income and more affluent families (Kahn & Kamerman, 1987).

Many remain skeptical regarding the chances for success of the 1988 reforms, especially the workfare component, because of the failure to address some of the broader, but more subtle obstacles to such efforts. The skeptics maintain that for those with only limited employment potential the program really offers little hope (Dobelstein, 1990). Low education levels, limited work experience, lack of self-esteem and self-discipline, problems of substance abuse, and other such factors make it doubly difficult for such trainees to find and hold jobs even after training. Dobelstein (1990) pointed out that over 60% of those currently receiving AFDC benefits have never worked or have not worked within 5 years of receiving AFDC assistance.

The nationally known child expert T. Berry Brazelton (1991) feels that most efforts to date have been counterproductive, simply providing money without real support. If such programs are to succeed, some of the old biases must be discarded. "If there is an implicit bias in the United States," argued Brazelton, "it is this: families should be self-sufficient and if they're not they deserve to suffer" (p. D1). Therefore, he continued, to qualify for help families must first be identified as failures. Treated as failures, charged Brazelton, people will act as failures. To succeed such aid programs have to first of all make people feel as if they are worthy of help. Children in poor families, claimed Brazelton, sense the hopelessness in their parents and therefore learn to fail. They have little or no support in their own endeavors. Citing Lisbeth and Daniel Schorr's study, Brazelton stated successful aid programs require these characteristics:

Help must be available at all times and in many different forms.

There must be provisions for meeting individual differences and needs.

The staff administering the programs must be trained and must develop trust among the recipients of assistance.

The program must be accepted in the local communities.

Solutions, he noted, will be expensive and they will not be easy. Programs such as Head Start and WIC have succeeded because they have reached out to families. Family members are educated together in these programs, and as their children succeed then parents also begin to feel successful. These are the types of programs, says Brazelton, that produce a more lasting effect.

Because the new program on the whole fails to address the need for a broad range of support services to underpin job training and the development of a sufficient pool of appropriate and adequately paying jobs, its potential for helping many leave the welfare rolls seems rather limited. It could be a step in the right direction, but it appears to stop substantially short of what is necessary to achieve self-sufficiency for those on welfare.

The 1988 act also fails to address directly some of the current inequities and inadequacies in AFDC. Although the federal government provides about two thirds of the funding, AFDC is still controlled largely by the individual states, with each determining its own funding formula and eligibility requirements. Recipients are allocated benefits according to each state's definition of needs. In 1989 the average monthly benefit per family ranged from $114 in Alabama to $616 in

Alaska (*World Almanac,* 1990). Not all of the states pay benefits at
100% of the needs level they themselves determine. In 1985, 23 states
paid benefits at 100%; 4 states and the District of Columbia paid 50%
or less of their established needs level. Consequently the benefits
received by most families leave them well below the poverty level.
Robert Greenstein and Isaac Shapiro of the Center on Budget and Policy
Priorities found that 32 states provided maximum benefits that were less
than one half of poverty level for a family of three (Kosterlitz, 1989c).
For 1987 the median benefit for a family of three was 55% of the official
poverty level. In the 1980s increases in most states' benefits lagged well
behind rises in the cost of living so that by 1988 only 16 states were
paying benefits above 80% of the poverty level for a family of three.
Cash payments to low-income families with children fell by 21% during
the 1980s ("2.2 million children pushed into poverty," 1991). Since
1970 AFDC benefits in real dollars have declined about 40% (De Parle,
1991, p. A-5). Most AFDC recipients are eligible for food stamps also,
but even with food stamps, in the mid-1980s, a family of three was at
about 73% of the poverty level. And from 1976 to 1988 the combined
value of the two dropped by 20% (Chisman & Pifer, 1987). These are
issues that serious efforts at welfare reform still need to address.

Conclusion

As Chisman and Pifer (1987) pointed out, many Americans quite
readily stereotype the poor as lazy and irresponsible. A nagging fear
that the poor will abuse welfare benefits has remained an innate suspi-
cion for many Americans, and widely publicized critiques such as
Charles Murray's (1984) *Losing Ground* and George Gilder's (1981)
Wealth and Poverty simply confirm and reinforce their natural suspi-
cions. Murray charged in his work that many poor women organized
their lives so as to become eligible for AFDC.
    Although little hard evidence supports the critics' charges that the
system is *the* problem, neither have the policies of the past been the
solution for most of the problems. Most recipients use AFDC for
temporary relief and relatively few become long-term dependents.
There *is* waste and inefficiency but little evidence of systematic and
widespread abuse. Costs have not been excessive: In 1988 about $20
billion was spent for AFDC benefits and food stamps, about 10% of

social services spending and 5% of the federal budget (Van Horn et al., 1989). On the down side, administrative costs are too high relative to benefits provided.

Although attracting less attention and debate, other shortcomings are more significant. The programs have had little success in reducing poverty among children. The poverty rate among those under age 18 has exceeded 20% since the early 1980s. In a study released in June 1991, the Washington, D.C.-based Children's Defense Fund (CDF) reported that in 1989, 12.6 million children—one of every five—lived in families with incomes below the poverty threshold of $12,700 for a family of four ("2.2 million children pushed into poverty," 1991). The CDF reported that during the decade of the 1980s, 2.2 million more children were pushed into poverty and that by 1989 there were 4.9 million U.S. children—more than two in every five poor children—who were in families with incomes of less than one half the official poverty level. Consequently, the United States has one of the highest poverty rates among children of any industrialized country—five times that of Switzerland or Sweden.

The CDF study went on to point out several widely held misconceptions concerning federal cash benefits programs. First, more than one half of the benefits from such social spending programs go to nonpoor families. In 1987 only $1 of every $12 spent on programs benefiting families with children went to poor families. Furthermore, concluded the study, welfare was not the main source of income for poor families. In 1989 most poor families with children had at least one member working and the paycheck, though meager, was the main source of family income. Neither are such poor families large: Two thirds of poor families with children have only two. Contrary to popular belief, the study also found that only 1 in 10 poor children is black and that more poor children live outside the large cities than in them ("2.2 million children pushed into poverty," 1991).

Another problem with even some of the more successful programs for children is inadequate and patchwork coverage. In 1979 out of each 100 poor children, 83.6 received AFDC benefits; by 1987 the ratio was 59.8 per 100 (see Table 6.6). A Census Bureau study concluded that cuts in AFDC benefits were a major factor in the growth of poverty rates for single-parent families in the 1980s (Kotz, 1984, p. 23; "The numbers game," 1989). The WIC program started in 1972, which has gained rather broad support, still served only 4.5 million or about 54% of those eligible by 1990. In 1991 the House proposed adding $350 million to

Table 6.6 Child Support Payments and Numbers of Recipients by Age and Race, 1985 (Women as of spring 1986. Covers civilian noninstitutional population. Child support data are for women with own children under 21 years of age present from absent fathers. Based on current Population Survey; see text, section 1 and Appendix III)

Recipiency Status of Women	Unit	Total[1]	Age			Race			Current Marital Status			
			18 to 29 Years	30 to 39 Years	40 Years and Over	White	Black	Hispanic[2]	Divorced[3]	Married	Single[4]	Separated
All Women, Total	1,000	8,808	2,887	3,614	2,307	6,341	2,310	813	3,045	2,322	2,009	1,363
Payments awarded[5]	1,000	5,396	1,288	2,547	1,561	4,476	839	342	2,492	1,904	370	567
Percent of total	(%)	61.3	44.6	70.5	67.7	70.6	36.3	42.1	81.8	82.0	18.4	43.1
Due child support payment in 1985	1,000	4,381	1,089	2,182	1,110	3,651	657	282	2,179	1,417	303	453
Received payment	1,000	3,243	777	1,605	861	2,722	473	192	1,637	970	231	382
Percent of due	(%)	74.0	71.3	73.6	77.6	74.6	72.0	68.1	75.1	68.5	76.2	84.3
Did not receive payment	1,000	1,138	312	578	249	929	184	90	541	447	72	71
Payments not awarded	1,000	3,411	1,599	1,066	746	1,865	1,471	471	553	418	1,639	776
Women With Incomes Below the Poverty Level in 1985, Total	1,000	2,797	1,419	920	458	1,569	1,190	414	795	180	1,159	646
Payments awarded[5]	1,000	1,130	469	485	176	787	322	100	572	121	207	221
Received payments in 1985	1,000	595	241	258	96	411	174	43	301	50	123	116
Did not receive payment	1,000	310	128	147	35	221	83	31	198	31	40	41
Payments not awarded	1,000	1,668	951	435	282	782	868	314	223	59	952	425

1 Includes other items, not shown separately. 2 Hispanic women may be of any race. 3 Remarried women whose previous marriage ended in divorce. 4 Never-married women.
5 Includes women who were not supposed to receive payments in 1985, not shown separately.
SOURCE: U.S. Bureau of the Census, *Current Population Reports*, series P-23, No. 154.

WIC spending to cover 20% more recipients. They proposed coverage for all those eligible over the next 5 years. A 1986 study found fewer than one half of all children under age 13 who lived in poverty covered by medicaid. Head Start, which President Bush recommended for a 28% increase in spending in FY 1991, reached only about 20% of those eligible. A 1987 study by the General Accounting Office concluded that current programs for women, infants, and children provided benefits for fewer than one half those who were eligible ("Committee plan would boost WIC spending," 1991).

Another aspect of current policies that also needs attention is their primarily reactive rather than proactive nature. Existing programs tend to help families and children only after there is a crisis and damage has already occurred. Earlier involvement is needed, and addressing root causes rather than the symptoms of problems. The Ford Foundation (1989b) reported, "We stand aside as large numbers of children are damaged intellectually and socially in the early years of their life, and then rush in with remedial programs and anti-crime measures when the inevitable consequences of such neglect occur" (p. 6). Brazelton (1991) observed that in general those families that suffer the most social stress receive the least social support.

To be more effective, programs that provide for earlier intervention and are more adequate in their coverage and comprehensive in their scope must be developed. The United States tends to be slow in developing responses to social issues. Brazelton (1990) charged, "We are the least family-oriented society in the civilized world" (p. D1). We pay a lot of lip service, but there is little real commitment at the national level to family issues. For example, the United States is the only Western industrial nation that does not have in place a national program to pay for parental leaves for parents of newborn or recently adopted children. This has just recently become an issue on the U.S. social policy agenda. Lisbeth Schorr (1988) listed the following as items that need to be addressed in developing effective policies in response to our child and family welfare needs: "prenatal care, intensive personal counseling for at risk families, enriched child care programs, welfare linked to work, intensive school tutoring for lagging students, guaranteed jobs or college for poor young people willing to commit to hard work and dedication to their goal."

All of this will require new thinking and new approaches. It will require a commitment to change throughout our society; a team effort will be necessary to break out of the current mold. Governments, churches, schools, interest groups, community leaders—all will have to work toward common goals. And policymakers must consider some serious reordering of priorities and weigh some trade-offs that may now be more acceptable than in the past. Some researchers have concluded that for as little as $1.5 billion in new spending we could eliminate poverty among children in the United States. In social spending that may appear as a sizeable amount. Viewed in other terms, it is less than the cost of one giant aircraft carrier or three stealth bombers. In light of the changing international situation, is it not time for our society to consider investing as much in the welfare of our future generations as we put into two or three costly weapons systems?

Many of the proponents of more aid for families see the issue more as one of will than economics. Brazelton (1991) said the problems could be addressed, "but we seem to have lost the will even to think about it" (pp. D1, D4). Noting that the National Commission on Children found the data on the plight of children was widely reported but rarely followed up by any action, Brazelton asked, "Are we really so cynical or are we afraid to face the problem?" (p. D4). U.S. leaders, he added, seem unable to recognize that the greatest threat to our society is from within and not external, in the breakdown of families and the growing numbers of poor. He concludes:

> I have begun to regard the growing neglect and poverty of the young as the biggest threat to the nation's future. . . . The anger and addictions of the impoverished and the harm being done to their children are a national crisis. If we want poor children—and therefore all children—to have a future in this country, we have no choice but to make families our top priority. (p. D4)

Other studies and reports echo these concerns. The National Institute of Justice concluded: "Grim findings such as these ought to move a nation. They undermine our future and promise to thwart even the best intentions to make America safer and more prosperous. A more substantial investment in society's human infrastructure is overdue" ("The perils of abuse," 1991, p. A8). In its report the House Select Committee on Children, Youth and Families (1989) proclaimed, "The test now is whether we are motivated to promote policies that we know can reverse these alarming trends in the 1990s, or whether we will enter the 21st century besieged by the worst effects of our failure" (p. xiii). The historian Michael Katz, writing of the decade ending the 19th century, described it in these words: "Throughout the country, by the 1890s, children had captured the energy and attention of social reformers with an intensity never matched in other periods of American history. Almost overnight, it seemed, children became the symbol of a resurgent reform spirit" (Taylor, 1991, p. A5). Paul Taylor, a social writer for the *Washington Post,* wrote in 1991: "Children stand in 1991—just as they did a century ago—as the fulcrum that can move society from an era of material self-absorption to an era of civic-minded governmental activism. The political momentum for such a shift has been building for some time" (p. A5). The question is, have we developed that "resurgent reform spirit" necessary to produce the tough policy decisions that are demanded?

7

The Continuing Search for Social Policies That Work

In 1935 President Franklin Roosevelt hailed the passage of the Social Security Act as laying the cornerstone for programs that would eliminate poverty and income insecurity for U.S. citizens. Almost three decades later, in January, 1964, President Lyndon Johnson announced, "This administration today here and now declares unconditional war on poverty in America" (Johnson, 1965). Both President Roosevelt's New Deal, with social security as a centerpiece, and President Johnson's War on Poverty substantially expanded federal efforts in the social welfare field; and although both achieved substantial success on several fronts, they failed to provide the ultimate solutions to some of our most perplexing social and economic problems. What lessons, if any, have we learned from our past efforts and where do we go from here?

Part of the difficulty in addressing social welfare issues stems from the frequently contradictory ideas and values held by those making up our extremely pluralistic society. These contradictions are manifested in virtually every aspect of social welfare policy, making value consensus difficult or impossible to achieve and sending mixed and confusing signals to the policymakers. Almost every American when asked would profess a firm belief in the Declaration of Independence and the Constitution's proclamations of the principles of equality, due process, and equal protection under

133

the law. But when you move from the idea to the translation of these concepts into political and economic realities through efforts such as affirmative action, equal employment opportunity, and income redistribution any consensus erodes quickly. Likewise, a majority of Americans have come to accept, even expect, the government to undertake far-ranging efforts to promote and protect the general welfare of its citizens. Again, it is when it comes to footing the bill for such undertakings that many citizens begin to have reservations. According to T. Berry Brazelton (1991), the prevalent bias among Americans, despite evidence to the contrary, is that those who are destitute deserve it. Consequently many Americans harbor a strong resentment against their tax dollars going to support those "freeloaders on welfare who won't work to support themselves and their families."

Similar dichotomies appear in other areas as well and frequently complicate the development of policies that would more accurately reflect and address changes occurring in our culture and society. Today, despite the fact that well over one half of U.S. mothers are working outside the home and the trend is growing, debate over child care and related social policies is plagued by the conflict between current reality and the traditional idea that "a mother's place is in the home taking care of her children." Although research indicates the continuing decline of the traditional family pattern, much of the policy debate continues to embrace such ideological stereotypes. The whole area of child welfare and aid to families has become so enmeshed with normative views of the traditional American family that it is next to impossible to discuss such policies free of efforts designed to restore the family to its idealized, traditional form. Governor Thompson's efforts in Wisconsin mentioned in the previous chapter reflect this traditional concept of the family. Similar patterns are manifested in the continuing debates over work and welfare. In the U.S. system policy decisions, particularly those addressing social welfare issues, are often heavily influenced by normative considerations that make purely rational analysis and response difficult.

Another problem with current social welfare efforts is that they either tend to produce or fail to address inequities in our society. From 1980 to 1990 effective tax rates for the poorest 20% of our population went up while declining for the wealthiest 20%. A major contributing factor was heavier reliance on regressive taxes such as those for social security and medicare. An American with an average annual income of $0.5 million or more pays an effective maximum tax rate of 33% whereas a welfare mother at the poverty level may pay an effective rate of 80%-90% of what she earns in excess of her ADFC payment (Kaus, 1990; Phillips, 1990). The effective tax rate—that is, the amount actually paid in taxes, not the rate set in the tax codes—for many of the nation's most profitable corporations, because of special tax breaks, is minimal; yet these companies do not hesitate to move to Mexico, Taiwan, or elsewhere, taking much-needed jobs with them if the economic setting looks more inviting. The home mortgage tax credit designed to encourage and assist persons in buying their own home provides 52% of its benefits to 17% of the population who earn $50,000 or more per year while the 58% who earn $30,000 or less get only 30% of the benefits under this incentive plan (Mariano, 1988).

Traditional American ideas of individualism and equalitarianism often clash in the realm of social welfare policies. Although we have made progress in reducing the inequities in some areas, many Americans still do not enjoy equal opportunity and equal benefits in our current system. Discrimination may have become much more subtle and less overt, but it remains an obstacle for many in our society. Blacks, native Americans, other minorities, and women still are more likely to encounter discrimination and encounter more obstacles to equal treatment and equal opportunity than white males. Economic benefits remain an area of marked inequity in their distribution. Poverty, hunger, and homelessness remain a stark reality for many in the world's most productive economy. Equity and fairness remain goals to be pursued more diligently, as the belief that these are attainable objectives for everyone is the glue that binds our democracy together.

Though federal social efforts have helped to lift millions out of poverty and kept others from falling into it, numerous inadequacies are apparent. The social security retirement insurance program, one of the most successful of the social welfare efforts, has guaranteed an economically brighter and more secure future for millions of elderly, but benefit levels still leave some at the lower end of the scale living in poverty. Gaps in the coverage of most social welfare programs remain substantial. At the height of the recession of the early 1980s, fewer than one third of those out of work were receiving benefits under unemployment insurance. Benefit levels in the means-tested programs have not been indexed; consequently in the average state the combined value of AFDC and food stamp benefits declined by 20% between 1976 and 1988, falling substantially behind increases in the cost of living index. The selectivity of most in-kind programs such as medicaid, food stamps, and housing vouchers substantially reduces their usefulness as alternatives to income maintenance as they provide no added discretionary income. Effectiveness is further reduced by the fact that most programs reach only a portion of their target population. Currently fewer than one half of those eligible for food stamps are actually receiving them. Only about 20% of the children in families eligible for Head Start are currently enrolled in the program; in 1986 more than 5 million U.S. workers were paid less than the minimum wage; about 55% of those eligible for supplemental security income receive benefits; and overall, according to a 1988 Congressional Budget Office study, about two thirds of the poor households that qualify for some assistance receive none. In a nation producing far more than necessary to feed all its citizens, we have allowed to develop what one observer has labeled a "soup kitchen society" in which many are hungry and malnourished. Adequate housing is a growing problem and increasing numbers—no one knows just how many—live on the streets, sleeping on park benches, in subways, public buildings, on heating grates, or wherever else they can find a spot. The so-called urban underclass—and the problem is not just urban—are barely touched by current programs that really offer little hope for breaking the cycle in which those in this class are trapped. New approaches must be developed to address effectively the needs of this class, a task posing probably the greatest challenge to traditional social welfare thinking and policies.

At the start of the 1990s there are 60 to 100 different programs that provide social insurance, public assistance, and other forms of aid aimed at raising the standard of living for the poor. Federal spending for these programs is over $490 billion annually. As the number, size, and spending for such programs have grown, a crazy quilt pattern of programs and benefits has emerged without any clear-cut definition of goals and overall coordination. The result is a tangle of programs, agencies, departments, rules, and guidelines that frequently produce either gaps or overlaps in programs and benefits, or worse, contradictory policies and objectives that end up penalizing those the programs are supposed to benefit. At the federal level, at least 11 different House committees, 10 Senate committees, and 9 executive departments and agencies are involved in the formulation and administration of social welfare programs. And, if this alone is not enough, yet another factor contributing to the difficulties in coordination and administration is the joint federal-state nature of many social welfare programs. All these elements added together produce an administrative structure that is so sprawling, dispersed, and complex that it inevitably defies effective direction and coordination of efforts. Instead, it produces bureaucratic jealousies, competition, and jurisdictional disputes; excessive and burdensome rules and regulations; overlapping and unclear responsibilities; and increased administrative costs and inefficiency.

This vast bureaucratic network also creates numerous problems for beneficiaries and potential beneficiaries and is a contributing factor to the low rates of participation in some programs. Many of those potentially eligible become confused and discouraged by the red tape and complex rules, regulations, and tests they must satisfy to participate. For those who are largely unskilled and poorly educated, confronting the complex bureaucracies of the social welfare system with all the forms, questions, and hours and days of waiting can be an overwhelming, even devastating experience. It takes tremendous patience and perseverance to get through this maze of agencies and requirements, and many of those who may need assistance most are the least capable of coping with the system. For some, accessibility can be a problem. Often the poor, elderly, disabled, or ill lack the mobility or means of transportation to go to a local or regional office to apply for benefits. The complexity of the system also contributes to confusion, delays, misinterpretation, and misapplication of rules that can be a great burden for those seeking or drawing benefits under these programs. For someone whose benefit check barely gets him/her through the month, a few days' or a week's delay can be disastrous. Those in the administering agencies do not always fully appreciate this.

It should be pointed out, there are those who contend that the decentralized approach provides more advantages than disadvantages. They feel the involvement of more committees, agencies, and levels of government provides greater access and broadens the bases of support and votes for the various programs. This approach also allows more direct focus on the individual programs and more specialization on the part of their supporters and administrators. It also keeps the administration of the programs closer to those who benefit most directly from them.

Another drawback to existing programs and policies is part perception and part reality. A problem for both participants and for the general public is that some social welfare programs, especially the social assistance programs, have an element of stigma attached. Some who are eligible decline to apply for means-tested programs because of the stigma of such programs in their own and the public's eyes. Critics no doubt exaggerate the disincentive aspect of welfare programs, but this is an aspect policymakers cannot simply ignore. Such programs must aid and encourage self-sufficiency, not discourage it. People and families too often must qualify as failures before they qualify for assistance under the existing approach. Also existing programs sometimes have a punitive aspect in that they may actually penalize those who are trying hardest to improve their own lot. One HUD program is designed to help economically disadvantaged students pursue a master's degree in community and economic development. A young mother, a single parent who clearly was a prime candidate under this program, ended up having to decline a fellowship and forego pursuing a master's degree because the Bureau of Social Services ruled that with her stipend she would be earning too much and would no longer be eligible for child care. Without child care her stipend was not enough to enable her to continue her education. Programs should not constitute disincentives, but they also must avoid punitive aspects that become obstacles to individual efforts and opportunities to advance socially and economically.

Future Directions

A former chairman of the Council of Economic Advisers, the economist Arthur Okun (1975), noted that U.S. society awards

> prizes that allow the big winners to feed their pets better than the losers can feed their children. Such is the double standard of a capitalist democracy, professing and pursuing an egalitarian political and social system and simultaneously generating gaping disparities in economic well-being. (p. 2)

It is these disparities and unfair aspects of our society and the existing programs and policies that future efforts at welfare reform must address more effectively.

Our social and economic systems still do not treat all citizens evenly and fairly. Although there are signs of some progress, the pace has been much too slow. From 1971 to 1987 the number of female state legislators grew from 344 to 1,160; about one of seven state legislators is female. But Congress remains largely a male bastion, with only 6% females. Blacks and Hispanics also have been elected in greater numbers, but still not proportionate to their numbers in the population. During the first 5 years following the adoption of the Voting Rights Act of 1965, the number of black elected officials rose from under 200 to more than 1,500. During the 1970s and 1980s the rate of increase slowed, and by 1990 there were about 8,000 elected black officeholders. In the fall of 1991 440 of 7,466 legislative seats were held by blacks, or 5.9%. Blacks constituted 11.1% of the population. Hispanics held 115 legislative seats, or 1.5%, compared to their proportion, 7.9%, of the total population. Numbers alone, however, provide an incomplete picture. Wielding power and influence and actually changing policies involves much more than just taking office. Although their numbers have increased, women, blacks, and Hispanics proportionally hold an even smaller share of leadership positions in policy-making bodies. In 1990 William Gray III was the number three leader in the Democratic party in the U.S. House of Representatives, the highest ranking black in Congress; five blacks held statewide offices in the 50 states; California and North Carolina had black speakers in their state legislatures; and Pete Rios, an Hispanic, was president of the Arizona Senate. Douglas Wilder was the first black governor in the nation, and Atlanta, Birmingham, New Orleans, Baltimore, New York, Detroit, Los Angeles, and Philadelphia had black mayors. But minorities still faced greater odds in gaining political success, positions of leadership, and influence. In his race for governor in Virginia, Wilder polled 40% of the white vote, an excellent effort, as it usually takes a strong black candidate to poll more than 20% of the votes cast by white voters. It is still rare for black candidates to win elections in constituencies that are less than 65% black (Germond & Witcover, 1990; Peirce, 1991b).

Although their numbers are growing, minority and women officeholders, especially legislators, still face an uphill struggle as far as their power and influence. They must learn the ropes, build support among the leaders and their colleagues, and learn the leaders' agenda. They start as outsiders who must work harder and longer to gain acceptance. Experience also seems to indicate that those who gain the most success work through the system and make common cause with colleagues to achieve policy goals. Those coming from the ranks of the civil rights and women's movements appear to have less success because they somehow are more threatening to the majorities with whom they must work to attain their policy objectives (Germond & Witcover, 1990; Peirce, 1991b). As these minority policymakers grow in number and especially as they move into positions of leadership, their influence on policies will increase. But in the 1990s, because few had acquired leadership status, their overall influence was still disproportionately low.

Another reason for the shortfall in many social policies has been their failure to address adequately patterns of inequity. Inequities in income distribution have not improved since World War II; in fact, from 1980 to 1990 the gap has widened. Current social policies and programs fail almost totally to address the problems of the working poor. In 1986 over 5 million Americans were paid less than the minimum wage, providing them only a poverty-level existence. Future policy efforts must address this issue and strike a proper balance between the benefit levels for those who are unable to work and those who can and do work. Policymakers are extremely wary of benefit levels that may make work unattractive to some (disincentive), but benefits that are too skimpy can cause the genuinely dependent to suffer. The equitable solution is to raise both the dependent and the working poor to levels that will provide an acceptable standard of living for both. This means serious consideration of approaches such as the negative income tax or guaranteed annual income. Those who seek to be self-sufficient should be encouraged, not discouraged.

The black sociologist Thomas Sowell (1990a) has been critical of black leaders for pushing approaches in social welfare that he charges have been counterproductive for most disadvantaged blacks. He asked: "Have the philosophies and policies so much supported by black leaders contributed to the decline in community and personal standards, and in family responsibility, so painfully visible today?" (p. 668). Again past policies have failed the poor because they have failed in large measure to address the root causes of their problems—high dropout rates and low educational levels; lack of basic job skills; high unemployment rates; low-paying, dead-end jobs; and discriminatory treatment. The consequence of these factors is that those from poor families are more likely to be unemployed and involved in crime in the 1980s than they were 20 years ago. According to the economist Robert Reich of Harvard University's John F. Kennedy School of Government, two of the fastest growing occupational groups in our nation in the 1990s were prison and security guard. In a study on social welfare policies, the Ford Foundation (1986b) warned: "We cannot build enough prisons or buy enough home security systems to protect our private worlds from the social decay that spreads when true opportunity is denied to large numbers of people" (p. 5).

New approaches must be developed to address the root causes of these problems and break the cycle that creates an attitude of resignation to a life of idleness and poverty. William Aramony, president of United Way, says, "We have the biggest single opportunity in our history to address 200 years of unfairness to blacks. If we don't, God condemn us for blowing the chance" (Peirce, 1989b, p. 809).

A successful response to our social problems and needs is going to require a much clearer sense of direction and definition of goals than has been reflected in past efforts. A good place to start would be with more realistic, clearer, and more precise definitions of "poverty" and "need." The measures now in use were adopted in the early 1960s and are based on data drawn from the 1950s. Many contend that these measures are sadly out of date and need a wholesale redefinition. Following hearings of the Joint Economic Committee in April 1990, Congressman Stephen J. Solarz (D., NY) announced, "It became clear during the course of our hearing that the current criterion for measuring poverty in the country is hopelessly out of date and does not, in fact, provide an accurate picture of poverty in the country" (Kosterlitz, 1990b, pp. 1982-1983). Some who are pushing for redefinition feel a revised poverty level could result in less polarization over the issue. Patricia Ruggles maintains that a poverty population that was more mainstream, that is, more white, more elderly, more two-parent families, more working poor, would make support more acceptable generally. "It's easier," she said, "for people to identify with those who are more mainstream" (*National Journal,* August 4, 1990, p. 1896). Without this, programs and their intended beneficiaries become enmeshed in a confusing tangle of rules that result in mistakes, unnecessary delays, and inequities. Americans in general and their policymakers must overcome their ambiguous attitudes toward social welfare and develop programs and policies based not on myths and perceptions but on the realities of current society.

Along with more clearly defined goals and objectives, successful policies will also require better coordination and administration. Current policies are a patchwork of uncoordinated and disjointed efforts spread across the governmental firmament. President Johnson took some steps toward a more coordinated approach, but his War on Poverty generated so much opposition that succeeding presidents were bent on dismantling its structure. Both Presidents Nixon and Reagan took steps to decentralize the administration of welfare programs in efforts to lower their profile and to reduce federal involvement. With as much of our national budget going into social welfare spending as now does, more centralized responsibility, direction, and control are warranted. Congress needs to redefine committee jurisdictions to reduce the number of committees involved and bring a more coordinated and unified approach to social welfare legislation. Administrative responsibility in the executive branch needs to be consolidated under one or at least as few departments and agencies as possible. And finally, if the federal government is going to continue the major funding of most of these programs—and it must if the programs are to continue at current levels—there must be more uniformity and centralized control and direction. In the interest of both adequacy and equity, eligibility requirements should be standardized and minimum benefit levels set nationally. Under the current decentralized and highly fragmented arrangement it is difficult or impossible to achieve any coordination of effort or clear sense of direction. Also any degree of responsibility and accountability is virtually out of the question.

Much policymaking in the U.S. system is on the incremental pattern; that is, policies are developed step by step in a piecemeal fashion. This has been the case with social welfare efforts, helping to produce the hodge-podge of programs and policies currently in place. But the complexity, scope, and interrelatedness of social issues necessitate a broader-based, more integrated and comprehensive response. Although some existing programs have worked fairly well for the kinds of problems addressed, they have been too piecemeal in their approach and have failed to address some of the more subtle and complex aspects of issues such as poverty, unemployment, and job discrimination. Future policies must address the highly complex social issues on a broader scale by putting together packages of services and benefits that will provide a more coordinated and comprehensive response to the needs of the target populations. Such packages would include education, literacy training, job training, job and marital counseling, family planning, financial counseling, job development, child care, health care, housing, and other services designed to help break not only the financial bonds but also the psychological bonds that so often bind those in need. To succeed, such social programs must provide opportunities that are real. All too often past efforts, such as jobs programs, have fallen short in this respect because many of the jobs available at the end of the programs were not adequate. Even though people went to work, they could not break out of the poverty cycle.

A major component of any response to the social welfare needs of the nation has to be improvement in the educational levels of those to be aided. Poverty and unemployment rates are considerably higher among those who have not finished high school than for those who have. Also the average lifetime earnings for high school graduates are substantially higher than for nongraduates. Frances Moore Lappe, author of *Rediscovering America's Values* (1989), pointed out that poverty's cost to society can also be measured in the loss of potential wealth. Each class of high school dropouts, she argued, represents roughly $240 billion in lost earnings and tax revenues alone (p. 33). Unless the educational levels of the labor force are improved, the increasing numbers of knowledge-intensive jobs will leave even more undereducated and inadequately trained workers behind. By the year 2000 almost three fourths of the current work force will require retraining (American Society for Training and Development, 1988). Even if our economy generates new jobs, unless the workers are better educated and trained, especially those struggling to escape poverty, they will not be in a position to benefit.

Although a mounting federal deficit makes it difficult to consider new spending initiatives, our lagging economy, declining productivity, and lack of competitiveness on the global economic front demand new approaches. In the decade following World War II the United States was the world's dominant economic power and steady economic growth was taken for granted. But by the mid-1960s other countries were experiencing more rapid economic growth than the United States and the spendable income of Americans was declining. By the 1970s the U.S. share of the world market for manufactured goods had dropped 25% and U.S. workers in the manufacturing sector saw their earnings fall below those of workers in several foreign countries (Van Horn, Baumer, & Gormley, 1989). Our initial response was more in the direction of propping up weak, noncompetitive producers than in developing policies that would promote a more competitive stance in the changing world economy. Such efforts are both shortsighted and nonproductive. For example, U.S. efforts to regulate trade to protect domestic producers and jobs have cost about $75,000 per job. Not very cost-effective.

A more effective and productive approach would be to consider a broad-based investment in human capital programs that would address our social welfare problems and productivity problems at the same time. One of the factors contributing to the decline in economic growth and productivity has been a skills shortage in the work force. By investing in comprehensive education, training, and support services for those unemployed and living in poverty, our country could help meet its labor needs, transform many of those who are now a burden on the economy into productive workers and consumers, and improve our competitive stance in the global marketplace. Only about 5% of all noncollege youth who are eligible for federally funded job training are actually receiving help under current programs. This is a waste of human capital resources we need to be developing.

The Joint Center for Political Studies (1990) made the case in these terms: "We urge a concentrated effort by government to invest first in models and then in programs and strategies for human development that will facilitate economic independence and encourage the poor to take charge of their own lives" (p. 674). Scott Fosler of the Committee for Economic Development expressed similar sentiments: "Here's our chance. Let's get these people into the workforce. We have people looking for work, employers who need them. Let's get them together" (Peirce, 1989b, p. 809). This approach is no panacea that would immediately solve all our economic and social welfare problems, but it could be a major step forward. Many of those who need help are unable to work and such an effort would not address their needs. Such a program would require a substantial investment and broad-based, long-term commitment on many fronts. It would require a team effort involving governments, interest and professional groups, business and industry, schools, churches, and other institutions all pulling in the same direction. In the past many interests have pushed for programs in particular areas, some for housing, some for food programs, others for jobs, and so forth. The focus of these programs has been too narrow, failing to address the full scope of the problem. It is time now to attack on a broader front and bring these diverse interests together in a more coordinated effort addressing the full range of social welfare issues.

In *The State and Democracy: Revitalizing America's Government,* the editor Marc Levine (1988) observed that with the Reagan era drawing to a close, debate over the proper role of government in our democratic society is opening up more. We can only hope as we move toward the 21st century that this increased willingness to debate such issues as the government's social welfare role will bring some long overdue reordering of social and economic priorities in our system. For decades our political leaders have used national security and economic arguments to mask a real lack of commitment to spending on social programs. At least three developments at the start of the 1990s should weaken the continued credibility of such arguments. First, changes in the Soviet Union and the subsequent "thawing" of the cold war should make continued claims for massive military spending considerably less compelling. To what extent this actually happens remains to be seen. President Bush's FY 1991 and FY 1992 budgets called for $307.8 billion and $300.4 billion respectively for defense and $199.8 billion and $212.0 billion for domestic programs. But despite the cold war thaw, he still requested $4.07 billion in FY 1991 and $5.25 billion in FY 1992 for the Star Wars defense system. Development Number 2: Despite concern over the spiraling national deficit, the government found funds for a massive bailout of a failed savings and loan system. Development Number 3: The president and Congress somehow found funds for an unprecedented military operation in the Persian Gulf, at a cost of $500 million to $1 billion per day. The Pentagon then spent at least $3 million just to welcome home returning troops (McGrory, 1991). So, as the nationally syndicated columnist Ellen Goodman wrote, "Americans seem to know what patriotism looks like in war. But we don't know what it looks like in peace" (p. A11). In the "Editor's Preface" to *The State and Democracy,* Chester Hartman (1988) wrote: "The problem . . . is not the inability to create workable alternatives, but our system's unwillingness to effect the basic economic, social and political changes in the structure of American society that will permit such alternatives to take root." Goodman (1991) said, "One thing we learned in the Gulf: If you have the will, you find the wallet, and the way" (p. A11).

A major lacking ingredient for effectively addressing our social welfare problems has been the will. Maybe if the cost of such an undertaking is viewed as an investment in developing a vital human capital resource rather than a costly expenditure for the support of nonproductive elements of our society, we can generate the necessary will to act. The question then becomes: Can we afford not to make such a vital investment in our future?

References

1980s called "terrible decade" for children in U.S. (1991, February 2). *Courier-Journal,* p. A2. (Louisville, KY).

2.2 million children pushed into poverty. (1991, June 3). *Daily News,* p. 6-A. (Bowling Green, KY).

Aaron, H. J. (Ed.). (1990). *Setting national priorities: Policy for the nineties.* Washington, DC: Brookings Institution.

AFL-CIO proposes federal jobs program. (1991, February 19). *Courier-Journal,* p. B6 (Louisville, KY).

Aid to poor seen as cost effective. (1985, August 19). *Washington Post,* p. A10.

American Society for Training and Development. (1988). *Gaining the competitive edge.* Alexandria, VA.

America's English disease. (1990, August, 16). *Courier-Journal* (Louisville, KY). (Reprinted from the *New York Times,* p. A11.)

Aprile, D. (1990, August 16). Homless get compassion more than other U.S. poor. *Courier-Journal,* pp. C1, C8.

At a glance. (1990, September 8). *National Journal,* p. 2144. (Louisville, KY).

Bagdikian, B. H. (1964). *In the midst of plenty.* Boston: Beacon.

Ball, K. (1991, January). Productivity plunges in 1990—First two-year drop in a decade. *Daily News,* p. 6-A (Bowling Green, KY).

Barone, M. (1990). *Our country: The shaping of America from Roosevelt to Reagan.* New York: Free Press.

Bawden, D. L., & Palmer, J. L. (1982). Social policy: Challenging the welfare state. In J. L. Palmer & I. Sawhill (Eds.), *The Reagan record,* pp. 177-215. Cambridge, MA: Ballinger.

Bender, D., & Leone, B. (Eds.). (1988). *The elderly: Opposing viewpoints.* San Diego, CA: Greenhaven.

Births among unmarried women concern researchers. (1991, February 2). *Courier-Journal,* pp. A7, A10. (Louisville, KY).

Bluestone, B., & Harrison, B. (1990). The great American machine: The proliferation of law—wage employment in the U.S. economy. In A. Serow, W. Shannon, & E. Ladd (Eds.), *The American polity reader* (pp. 615-619). New York: Norton.

Bradwell v. Illinois, 16 Wallace 131 (1873).

Brazelton, T. B. (1991, January 13). Is America failing its children? *Courier-Journal* (Louisville, KY). (Reprinted from *The New York Times Magazine,* pp. D1, D4.)

Burtless, G. (1989). In P. Cottingham & D. Ellwood (Eds.), *Welfare policy for the 1990s.* Cambridge, MA: Harvard University Press.

Bush, G. (1989, June). [Acceptance Speech]. Republican National Convention, New Orleans.

Children of poverty. (1989, May 27). In The numbers game. *National Journal,* p. 1325.

Chisman, F., & Pifer, A. (1987). *Government for the people: The federal social role, what it is, what it should be.* New York: Norton.

Citizens Commission on Hunger in New England. (1984, February). *Report.*

City of Richmond v. Croson, 102 L.Ed. 2d 854 (1989).

Clark, T. (1987a, February 14). Hewers of wood. *National Journal,* p. 399.

Clark, T. (1987b, March 21). Raising the floor. *National Journal,* p. 702.

Cochran, C., Mayer, L. Carr, T. R., & Cayer, J. N. (1990). *An introduction: American public policy.* New York: St. Martin's.

Committee plan would boost WIC spending. (1991, April 14). *Daily News,* p. 11-C (Bowling Green, KY).

Conference on the trend in income inequality in the U.S. report. (1977). Institute of Research on Poverty, Madison: University of Wisconsin.

Congress and the Nation. (1969). Vol. 2. Washington, DC: Congressional Quarterly Press.

Congress and the Nation, 1985-1988. (1989). Washington, DC: Congressional Quarterly Press.

Congress and the Nation, 1945-1964. (1965). Washington, DC: Congressional Quarterly Press.

County of Washington v. Gunther, 452 U.S. 161 (1981).

Courier-Journal (Louisville, KY), various issues.

Craig v. Borden, 429 U.S. 190 (1976).

Decline in "married-with-children" lifestyle slowed in U.S. during '80s. (1991, January 30). *Courier-Journal,* p. A3. (Louisville, KY).

DeParle, J. (1988, March). . . . and start helping the underclass. *Washington Monthly, 20,* 52-56.

DeParle, J. (1991, May 14). Reforming welfare. *Courier-Journal,* p. A5. (Louisville, KY).

Dobelstein, A. *Social welfare: Policy and analysis.* Chicago: Nelson-Hall.

Duston, D. (1991, April 14). Poor nutrition causes problems in elderly. *Daily News,* p. 11-C. (Bowling Green, KY).

Eagleton, T. (1982, July). Programs worth saving. *The Atlantic,* pp. 8-9, 12, 18-19.

Eskey, K. (1990). The elderly's wealth is not exaggerated. In D. Bender and B. Leone (Eds.), *The elderly: Opposing viewpoints* (pp. 85-89). San Diego, CA: Greenhaven.

Field Foundation. (1977). *Hunger in America: The federal response.* (2nd Report of the Physician's Task Force on Hunger, p. 47). San Diego, CA: Greenhaven.

Firefighters' Local Union 1784 v. Stotts, 104 S.Ct. 2576 (1984).

Ford Foundation. (1989a) *A proper inheritance: Investing in self-sufficiency of poor families.* Washington, DC.

Ford Foundation. (1989b). *The common good: Social welfare and the American future.* (Ford Foundation Project on Social Welfare and the American Future, Policy Recommendations of the Executive Panel). New York.

Ford Foundation. (1989c). *Work and family responsibilities: Achieving a balance.* New York.

Friedan, B. (1983). *The feminine mystique.* New York: W. W. Norton.

Frontiero v. Richardson, 411 U.S. 677 (1973), p. 685.

Fullilove v. Klutznick, 448 U.S. 448 (1980), pp. 523-525.

Fulton, D. (1986, August). Hands across America: An on-going link. *The World and I,* pp. 98-102.

Germond, J., & Witcover, J. (1990, March 10). American politics still far from colorblind. *National Journal,* p. 592.

Gilder, G. (1981). *Wealth and poverty.* New York: Basic Books.

Gilder, G. (1990). The nature of poverty. In A. Serow, W. Shannon, & E. Ladd (Eds.), *The American polity reader* (pp. 658-663). New York: Norton.

Goodman, E. (1991, April 9). Wallets and will. *Courier-Journal,* p. A11. (Louisville, KY).

Graham, G. G. (1985, Winter). Searching for hunger in America. *Public Interest, 77-80,*(78), 3.

Griggs v. Duke Power Company, 401 U.S. 424 (1971).

Guskind, R., & Steinbach, C. (1991, April 6). Sales resistance. *National Journal,* p. 798.

Harrington, M. (1990). The invisible land: Poverty in America from The Other America.. In A. Serow, W. Shannon, & E. Ladd (Eds.), *The American polity reader* (pp. 649-657). New York: Norton.

Hartman, C. (1988). *The state and democracy.* New York: Routledge.

Haveman, R. (1987). *Poverty policy and poverty research.* Madison: University of Wisconsin Press.

Helping teenage mothers who marry is plan's goal. (1991, February 26). *Daily News,* p. 6-A. (Bowling Green, KY).

Henig, J. (1985). *Public policy and federalism: Issues in state and local politics.* New York: St. Martin's.

Herson, L.J.R. (1990). *The politics of ideas: Political theory and American public policy.* Prospect Heights, IL: Waveland.

Hoyt v. Florida, 368 U.S. (1961).

Hungry children cannot learn. (1991, December-January). *Intercom,* p. 4.

Income gap between U.S. rich, poor widened in Reagan years. (1990, July 25). *Daily News,* p. 14-B. (Bowling Green, KY). (Based on report by the Center on Budget and Policy Priorities, Washington, DC).

Infofile. (1990a, March 31). *National Journal,* p. 807.

Infofile. (1990b, June 2). *National Journal,* p. 1368.

Infofile: Immigration. (1990, September 8). *National Journal,* p. 2159.

Jencks, C. (1988, June 13). Deadly neighborhoods. *New Republic, 198,* pp. 23-32.
Job-seeking pairs find discrimination in hiring. (1991, May 15). *Courier-Journal,* p. A5. (Louisville, KY).
Johnson, L. (1965). State of the union address. *Public papers of the presidents: Lyndon B. Johnson, 1963-1964,* V.I, p. 114. Washington, DC: Government Printing Office.
Johnson v. Transportation Agency, Santa Clara County, 107 S.Ct. 1442 (1987).
Joint Center for Political Studies. (1990). The black community's values as a basis for action. In A. Serow, W. Shannon, & E. Ladd (Eds.), *The American polity reader* (pp. 665-669). New York: Norton.
Kahn, A., & Kamerman, S. (1987). *Child care: Facing the hard choices.* Dover, MA: Auburn House.
Kahn v. Shevin, 416 U.S. 351 (1974).
Kaus, M. (1990, May 7). For a new equality. *New Republic,* pp. 18-27.
Kirschten, D. (1990a, August 11). A patchwork, not a policy. *National Journal,* p. 1980.
Kirschten, D. (1990b, March 3). Immigration focus. *National Journal,* p. 537.
Kondratas, A. (1986, August). Holding hands against hunger: How Americans were conned. *The World and I,* p. 97.
Kondratas, A. (1988). Hunger is not epidemic. In D. Bender & B. Leone (Eds.), *Poverty: Opposing viewpoints* (pp. 50-54). San Diego, CA: Greenhaven.
Kosterlitz, J. (1987a, September 19). Fading fathers. *National Journal,* p. 2337.
Kosterlitz, J. (1987b, February 28). They're everywhere. *National Journal,* p. 493.
Kosterlitz, J. (1988a, April 16). Family cries. *National Journal,* p. 994.
Kosterlitz, J. (1988b, December 10). Young v. old. *National Journal,* p. 3160.
Kosterlitz, J. (1989a, November 18). Costly cushion. *National Journal,* p. 2824.
Kosterlitz, J. (1989b, January 10). Personal histories of hard times. *National Journal,* p. 90.
Kosterlitz, J. (1989c, May 6). Society's child care. *National Journal,* p. 1110.
Kosterlitz, J. (1990a, February 17). Beefing up food stamps. *National Journal,* p. 389.
Kosterlitz, J. (1990b, August 4). Meaning misery. *National Journal,* pp. 1982-1993.
Kosterlitz, J. (1990c, September 8). No home, no help. *National Journal,* p. 2120.
Kotz, N. (1978, November 25). Feeding the hungry. *New Republic,* p. 22.
Kotz, N. (1984, April 30). The politics of hunger. *New Republic,* p. 20.
Lappe, F. M. (1989) *Rediscovering America's values.* New York: Ballantine.
Lawson, G. (1990, October 1). Job program aims to boost recipients off welfare rolls. *Courier-Journal,* p. A1. (Louisville, KY).
Levine, M. (Ed.). (1988). *The state and democracy: Revitalizing America's government.* New York: Routledge.
Light, P. C. (1985). *Artful work: The politics of social security reform.* New York: Random House.
Local 28 of the Sheetmetal Workers' International Assn. v. EEOC, 106 S.Ct. 3019 (1986).
Longman, P. (1985, June). Justice between generations. *Atlantic Monthly,* pp. 73-81.
Longman, P. (1987). *Born to pay.* Boston: Houghton Mifflin.
Lowi, T. (1979). *The end of liberalism.* (2nd ed.) New York: Norton.
Making ends meet with part-time work. (1990, October 27). *National Journal,* p. 2624.
Mann, T. (1990). Breaking the political impasse. In H. J. Aaron (Ed.), *Setting national priorities: Policy for the nineties* (pp. 293-317). Washington, DC: Brookings Institution.
Manpower Demonstration Research Corporation. (1980). *Summary and findings of the National Supported Work Demonstration.* Cambridge, MA: Ballinger.

Mariano, A. (1988, October 24-30). Is it a mortgage deduction or a housing subsidy for the wealthy? *Washington Post National Weekly Edition*, p. 20.

McGory, M. (1991, May 30). Memorial day rhetoric. *Courier-Journal*, p. A8. (Louisville, KY).

Metro Broadcasting v. FCC, 58 U.S.L.W. 5053 (1990), p. 5066.

Millett, K. (1990). *Sexual politics*. New York: S&S Trade.

Minkler, M. (1990). Poverty among the elderly is underestimated, *The Elderly*, p. 98.

Moore, W. J. (1990, June 23). After the marching. *National Journal*, p. 1528.

Morely, J. (1988, February 13). The new anti-poverty debate. *Nation, 246*, pp. 196-198.

Morris, M., & Williamson, J. B. (1986). *Poverty and public policy: An analysis of federal intervention efforts*. Westport, CT: Greenwood.

Murray, C. (1984). *Losing ground: American social policy, 1950-1980*. New York: Basic Books.

National Housing Preservation Task Force. (1988, February 15). [Report].

National Journal. various issues.

Navarro, P. (1984). *The policy game: How special interests and ideologues are stealing America*. Lexington, MA: Lexington.

Nixon, R. (1971). Address to the nation on domestic programs, August 8, 1969. *Public papers of the presidents: Richard Nixon, 1969*, pp. 637-638. Washington, DC: Government Printing Office.

Nixon, R. (1971). Special message to the congress recommending a program to end hunger in America, May 6, 1969. *Public papers of the presidents: Richard Nixon, 1969*, p. 350. Washington, DC: Government Printing Office.

Okun, A. (1975). *Equality and efficiency: The big tradeoff*. Washington, DC: Brookings Institution.

Peirce, N. (1988, January 16) A coalition approach to helping the homeless. *National Journal*, p. 138.

Peirce, N. (1989a, August 19). A national housing program that really works. *National Journal*, p. 2101.

Peirce, N. (1989b, April 1). A window of opportunity for black Americans. *National Journal*, p. 809.

Peirce, N. (1991a, March 19). Financing low-income housing. *Courier-Journal*, p. A8. (Louisville, KY).

Peirce, N. (1991b, January 5). Minorities slowly gain state offices. *National Journal*, p. 33.

Peterson, P. (1988). *On borrowed time: How the growth in entitlement spending threatens America's future*. ICS Press.

Phillips, K. (1990). *The politics of rich and poor*. New York: Random House.

Physicians Task Force on Hunger. (1985). *Hunger in America: The growing epidemic*. Wesleyan University Press.

Physicians Task Force on Hunger. (1988). Hunger is epidemic. In D. Bender & B. Leone (Eds.), *Poverty: Opposing viewpoints* (pp. 45-48). San Diego: Greenhaven.

Plan to free welfare moms from poverty lags. (1991, February 19). *Courier-Journal* (Louisville, KY).

Polit, D., & O'Hara, J. (1989). In P. Cottingham & D. Ellwood (Eds.), *Welfare policy for the 1990s*. Cambridge, MA: Harvard University Press.

Pollack, R. F. (1990). The elderly's wealth is exaggerated. In D. Bender and B. Leone (Eds.), *The elderly: Opposing viewpoints* (pp. 79-84). San Diego, CA: Greenhaven.

Productive u-turn: Corrected report shows worker efficiency up. (1991, May 7). *Courier-Journal*, p. C1. (Louisville, KY).

Purcell, D. (1991, February 7). Child care situation still causes problems. *Daily News*, p. 6-A. (Bowling Green, KY).

Rauch, J. (1988, April 16). Out of reach. *National Journal*, p. 1039.

Rauch, J. (1989, August 12). Downsizing the dream. *National Journal*, p. 2042.

Reed v. Reed, 404 U.S. 71 (1971).

Reich, R. (1991, February 3). Sobering words. [Address to College and University Administrators' meeting, Palm Beach, Florida]. (Reported in *Parade Magazine*, p. 12)

Reich, R. (1991, February 3). The fortunate fifth. *Courier-Journal Magazine*, pp. 14-15. (Louisville, KY).

Review of the News. (1978, May 3). [Interview with Orrin Hatch].

Riemer, D. R. (1988). *The prisoners of welfare*. Westport, CT: Praeger.

Rosen, D. P. (1989). *Public capital: Revitalizing America's communities*. Washington, DC: National Center for Policy Alternatives.

Rowan, C. (1991, May 14). Rescued by Job Corps. *Courier-Journal*, p. A4. (Louisville, KY).

Schlesinger, A. M., Jr., (1986). *The cycles of American history*. Boston: Houghton Mifflin.

Schneider, E. & Guralnik, J. M. (1990, May 2). The aging of America: Impact on health care costs. *Journal of the AMA*.

Schorr, L. (1988). *Within our reach: Breaking the cycle of disadvantage*. New York: Doubleday.

Schwarz, J. E. (1988). *America's hidden success: A reassessment of public policy from Kennedy to Reagan*. New York: Norton.

Segalman, R., & Marsland, D. (1989). *Cradle to grave: Comparative perspectives on the state of welfare*. New York: St. Martin's.

Sheltered forever. (1991, February 22). *Courier-Journal* (Louisville, KY).

Sowell, T. (1981). *Markets and minorities*. New York: Basic Books.

Sowell, T. (1990a). Civil rights: Rhetoric or reality? In A. Serow, W. Shannon, & E. Ladd (Eds.), *The American polity reader*. New York: Norton.

Sowell, T. (1990b). The special case of blacks. From Civil Rights: Rhetoric or reality? In A. Serow, W. Shannon, & E. Ladd (Eds.), *The American Polity Reader* (pp. 664-668). New York: Norton.

State jobless rate fell to 7.3% in April. (1991, May 30). *Courier-Journal* (Louisville, KY).

Steinbach, C. (1988, December 17). Those points of light. *National Journal*, p. 3192.

Steinbach, C. (1989, April 8). Shelter-skelter. *National Journal*, p. 851-855.

Steinbach, C. (1990a, March 10). The hourglass market. *National Journal*, pp. 568-572.

Steinbach, C. (1990b, October 27). The numbers game: Making ends meet with part time work. *National Journal*, p. 2624.

Steinbach, C., & Peirce, N. (1987, June 6). Picking up hammers. *National Journal*, p. 1464-1468.

Stone, M. E. (1990, September 8). Economic Policy Institute report. *National Journal*, p. 2159.

Study details struggle of needs for proper diet. (1991, March 27). *Courier-Journal*, p. A-2. (Louisville, KY).

Survey finds one in eight children hungry. (1991, March 26). *Daily News*, p. 6-A. (Bowling Green, KY).

Taylor, P. (1991, June 12). Tax policy and children. *Courier-Journal,* p. A5. (Louisville, KY).

The numbers game. (1990, March 31). *National Journal,* p. 806.

The perils of abuse. (1991, February 19). *Courier-Journal,* p. A8. (Louisville, KY).

Unemployment protection said at unparalleled low. (1991, April 4). *Daily News,* p. 1-A. (Bowling Green, KY).

United Steelworkers of America v. Weber, 443 U.S. 193 (1979).

University of California Regents v. Bakke, 438 U.S. 265 (1978).

U.S. Bureau of the Census. (1990). *Statistical abstract of the United States* (110th Ed.). Washington, DC: Author.

U.S. Bureau of the Census. (1991). *Statistical abstract of the United States* (111th Ed.). Washington, DC: Government Printing Office.

U.S. Congress, House Select Committee on Children, Youth and Families. (1989, September). *U.S. children and their families: Current conditions and recent trends, 1989.* (Report No. 21-956, 101st Congress, 1st Session) Washington, DC: Government Printing Office.

Van Horn, C., Baumer, D., & Gormley, W. T., Jr. (1989). *Politics and public policy.* Washington, DC: Congressional Quarterly Press.

Victor, K. (1990a, April 14). Helping the haves. *National Journal,* p. 901.

Victor, K. (1990b, June 23). Injured system. *National Journal,* p. 1537.

Wagman, R. J. (1991, April 10). Welfare cuts: California's poor may get poorer. *Daily News,* p. 6-A. (Bowling Green, KY).

Wards Cove Packing Company v. Atonio, 109 S.Ct. 2115 (1989).

Weisbrot, R. (1990). *Freedom bound: A history of the civil rights movement.* New York: Norton.

Wicker, T. (1991, May 31). A time for action. *Courier-Journal,* p. A9. (Louisville, KY).

WIC works. (1991, April 9). *Courier-Journal* (Louisville, KY). (Reprint of editorial from the *New York Times,* p. A11.)

Wilson, D. L. (1990a, July 28). About that great American dream. *National Journal,* p. 1857.

Wilson, D. L. (1990b, July 14). Death at an early age in the United States. *National Journal,* p. 1743.

Wilson, D. L. (1990c, June 23). U.S. melting pot is still bubbling. *National Journal,* p. 1565.

Wilson, W. J. (1987). *The truly disadvantaged.* Chicago: University of Chicago.

Wilton, D. L. (1990, August 18). America's Hispanics are falling behind. *National Journal,* p. 2033.

World almanac and book of facts, 1991. (1990). New York: Pharos Books.

Wright, J., & Dwyer, E. (Eds.). *The American almanac of jobs and salaries.* New York: Avon.

Wygant v. Jackson Board of Education, 106 S.Ct. 1842 (1986).

Index

Aaron, H., 16
Abernathy, R., 42
Act for Better Child Care Services, 6, 123
Adkins v. Children's Hospital, 107
Affirmative action, 13, 79, 96, 97, 134, 135
Age Discrimination Act, 96
Agriculture, Committee on, 43, 56
Agriculture, Department of, 56
Agriculture Trade Act of 1935, 52
Aid to Families with Dependent Children,
    13, 19, 36, 39, 51, 78, 113, 116-118,
    119-127, 135
Aid to the aged. *See* Supplemental Security
    Income
Aid to the blind. *See* Supplemental Secu-
    rity Income
Aid to the disabled. *See* Supplemental Se-
    curity Income
American Legion, 58
American Psychological Association, 58

Americans for Generational Equity, 9, 39
Andrews, M., 46
Annie E. Casey Foundation, 123
Apgar, W. C., Jr., 59
Appalachian development, 27
Aramony, W., 141

Bach, R., 105
Bagdikian, B., 26
Bailey v. Drexel Furniture Company, 107
Barone, M., 15
Berger, R., 4
Bertini, C., 48
Bill of Rights, 92
Block grants, 4, 66
Bradley, J., 92
Bradwell, v. Illinois, 92
Brazelton, T. B., 125-126, 130, 131, 134
Brennan, W. J., 92, 97

Bryant, J., 104
Bush, G., viii, 5, 14, 16, 26, 52, 66, 67, 70,
    71, 81, 91, 98, 106, 106, 122, 123,
    124, 130, 145
Business roundtable, 6

Campbell, D. 74
Capital gains tax, 26
Capital investment, 15
Carter, J., 69, 86, 121
CBS, 42
Center for the Study of Social Policy, 123
Center on Budget and Policy Priorities, 86
Chamber of Commerce, U.S., 6, 81
Child care, 11, 79, 92, 116, 122-23, 134
Child labor, 118
Child Nutrition Act of 1966, 52
Children, 22
Children's Bureau, 118
Children's Defense Fund, 58, 123, 128
Child support, 112-13, 121
Child Support Enforcement Program, 113
Child Trends, 78
Chisman, F., 5, 9
Citizen's Board of Inquiry into Hunger and
    Malnutrition, 42
Citizen's Commission on Hunger in New
    England, 44
Citizen's Crusade Against Poverty, 42
City of Richmond v. Croson, 98
Civilian Conservation Corps, 82
Civil rights, 4, 13, 95, 98, 105
Civil Rights Act
    of 1990, 98, 106
    of 1972, 96
    of 1964, 95, 96
Clay, P., 61
Clay, W., 67
Coalition on Human Needs, 11, 78
Collective bargaining, 76, 82
Commission to Prevent Infant Mortality, 115
Committee on Economic Security, 3
Committee on School Lunch Participation,
    42
Commodities distribution. See Food Stamps
Community Action Agencies, 28, 30, 40
Community development, 4

Community Development Block Grants
    Program, 69, 73
Community Development Corporations,
    72, 73
Comparable worth. See Pay equity
Comprehensive Employment Training act,
    78, 89, 96
Congress, 16, 19, 32, 33, 43, 51, 57, 59, 67,
    69, 70, 71, 74, 81, 86, 88, 91, 96, 106,
    113, 118, 121, 122, 123, 124, 142
Congressional Budget Office, 48, 103, 104, 114
Conservatives, 6, 38, 43, 45, 47, 48, 65, 66,
    78, 79, 87, 115, 116, 117, 120, 124-125
Constable, W., 78
Constitution, U.S., 2
Cooper, J. F. 2
Cost of Living Adjustments, 34
Council of Economic Advisors, 9
Council on competitiveness, 14
County of Washington v. Gunther, 102
Craig v. Boren, 100
Cranston, A., 74
Crime Control Act, 96
Cuomo, M., 125

Davis-Bacon Act, 80
Declaration of Independence, 1, 92, 133
Democratic convention, 125
DeParle, J., 79
Disability insurance, 4, 13, 33, 78
Disaster Relief Act, 96
Discrimination, 135, 142
Discriminatory effect, 97, 106
Discriminatory intent, 97, 106
Disincentive, 11, 78, 117, 122, 138, 140
Divorce rate, 14, 109-110, 111
Dobelstein, A., 20, 79
Domenici, P., 59
Donahue, J., 90
Downey, T. J., 81, 124
Downs, A., 75
Durenberger, D., 39
Dwyer, J., 55

Eagleton, T., 10
Economic Opportunity Act, 27

Economic Policy Institute, 84, 90
Economic system, U.S., 2, 10
Education and Labor, Committee on, 12, 88, 124
Elderly, 8-9, 12, 22, 37, 38, 52, 55, 135
Elementary and Secondary Education Act, 28
Employment, 40, 76-107
Energy crisis, 13
Entitlement programs, 6, 8, 75
Equal Employment Act, 96
Equal Employment Opportunity Commission, 95, 96, 105-106
Equality, 10, 92, 106, 133
Equal opportunity, 5, 10, 76, 79, 92-102, 106, 134, 135
Equal Pay Act, 95, 101

Fair Labor Standards Act, 80, 119
Family, 7, 8, 14, 113
Family Assistance Plan, 121
Family income, 23-24
Family programs, 108-132
Family Support Act of 1988, 121
Farmer's Home Administration, 67, 68
Faux, J., 90
Federal Contract Compliance Program, 106
Federal Emergency Management Administration, 71
Federal Home Loan Banks, 73
Federal Home Loan Mortgage Association, 68
Federal Housing Administration, 15
Federal National Mortgage Association, 68
Fefferman, H., 67
"Feminization" of poverty, 114
Fersh, R., 45
Field Foundation, the, 41, 43, 49-50
Firefighters' Local Union 1784 v. Stotts, 98
Fleming, A., 39
Food assistance programs, 44
Food Research and Action Center, 45
Food Stamp Act, 50
Food stamps, 3, 4, 7, 27, 28, 36-37, 46, 49, 50, 51-52, 78, 127, 135-136
Forbes, 8
Ford Foundation, the, 3, 12, 109, 111, 130, 140

Fosler, S., 144
Fourteenth Amendment, 92, 96, 106n
Free enterprise, 1, 4, 5, 100
Freeman, O., 42
Freemarket. *See* Free enterprise
Freidan, B., 100
Freidman, M., 9
Frontiero v. Richardson, 92, 100
Fullilove v. Klutznick, 96, 97

General Accounting Office, 60
General Dynamics, 9
GI Bill, 3, 15, 77, 87
Gilder, G., 6, 7, 8, 13, 127
Global competition, 15, 16, 106, 143-144
Goldfinger, S., 64
Goldwater, B., Sr., 39
Goodman, E., 145
Government National Mortgage Association, 68, 73
Graham, G., 46, 47,
Gray, W. III, 139
Great Depression, 2, 3, 4, 16, 67, 76, 79-80
Great Society, the, 41, 43, 95
Greenspan Commission, 32
Greenstein, R., 127
Griggs v. Duke Power Company, 97
Grogan, P., 72

Habitat for Humanity, 69
Hammer v. Dagenhart, 107n
Harper, V., 57
Harrington, M., 12, 26, 41
Hartman, C., 145
Hatch, O., 5
Hawkins, A., 12
Head Start, 27, 123, 126, 130, 136
Health and Human Services, Department of, 112-13, 118
Henig, J., 29
Heritage Foundation, the, 6, 25
Herson, L., 14
Homeless, 70
Homeless Assistance Act of 1987, 71
Homeless Service Network, 71
Home ownership, 61-62, 63-64

Home Ownership and Opportunity for People Everywhere, 66
Hopelessness, 54-75, 136
Hoover Institute, the, 6
House Select Committee on Children, Youth and Families, 112, 125, 131
Housing, 4
Housing Act:
  of 1954, 68
  of 1937, 67
Housing Act Amendments:
  of 1957, 68
  of 1968, 69
Housing and Urban Development, Department of, 57, 64, 69, 72, 73
Housing rehabilitation, 68, 69
Hoyt, v. Florida, 92
Hunger, 41-56

Immigrants, 104
Immigration Reform and Control Act, 105
Income maintenance, 12, 30-31, 33, 36, 89, 90, 102, 108, 120, 121, 136
Income tax credits, 36
Indexing, 34
Individualism, 1, 4, 5, 135
Infant mortality rate, 114-115
In-kind benefits, 7, 11, 36-37, 75, 135
Interagency Council on the Homeless, 71
Interfaith Coalition Against Hunger, 43
ITT, 9

Job Corps, 27, 28, 78, 88-89
Job Opportunities and Basic Skills (JOBs), 91, 122
Job segregation, 101
Job training, 4, 11, 29, 76, 77-78, 82, 87-91, 102, 121-122, 126, 144
Job Training and Partnership Act, 90
Johnson, Lyndon B., 3, 26, 27, 29, 50, 69, 88, 95, 133, 141
Johnson v. Transportation Agency, Santa Clara County, 97
Joint Center for Housing Studies, 60
Joint Center for Policy Studies, 144
Joint Economic Committee, 141

Kahn v. Shevin, 100
Katz, M., 131-32
Kemp, J., 66, 67, 72
Kennedy, A., 97
Kennedy, E., 81
Kennedy, J. F., 27, 50, 88, 95
Kennedy, R. F., 43
King, M. L., 99
Kondratas, A., 46, 47
Kosters, M., 114
Kristol, I., 6

Labor and Public Welfare, Committee on, 42, 43, 81
Ladner J., 124
Landrum-Griffin Act, 82
Lappe, F. M., 143
"Latchkey" kids, 116
Leadership, 16, 56, 144
League of Women Voters, 43
Legal services, 28
Levine, M., 144
Levitan, S. A., 17, 90
Liberals, 9-13, 47, 65-66, 79, 98, 117, 125
Light, P., 32
Lilly Foundation, Eli, 72
Lincoln, A., 9
Local Initiatives Support Corporation, 72
Local 28 of the Sheetmetal Workers International Association v. EEOC, 9
Longman, P., 38
Lowi, T., 29

Mann, T., 16, 17
Manpower Demonstration Research Corporation, 79
Manpower Development Training Act, 88
Marsland, D., 7
Mayer, A., 81
Mayer, J., 124
McGovern, G., 43
McMurray, G., 69
Medicaid, 7, 13, 19, 28, 91, 122, 130, 135
Medicare, 12, 13, 19, 28, 33, 134
Meissner, D., 105
Metro Broadcasting v. FCC, 97

Middle class, 12, 15, 19, 24, 40
Miller, J. C., III, 38
Millett, K., 100
Minimum wage, 80, 136, 140
Minkler, M., 9
Minorities, 8, 23, 30, 93, 96, 99, 105, 135, 139
Model Cities program, 69
Moody, J., 39
Morrison, B., 105
Moynihan, D., 32
Muntz, J., 72
Murphy, G., 42
Murray, C., 6, 13, 127

National Association of Home Builders, 58, 63
National Association of Manufacturers, 6
National Bureau of Economic Research, 6
National Coalition for the Homeless, 58
National Commission on Children, 123, 131
National Commission on State Workmen's Compensation Laws, 86
National Community Development Initiative Effort, 72
National Council of Churches, 43
National Council on Hunger, 43
National deficit, 14, 20, 32, 72, 74, 143
National Institute of Justice, 123, 131
National Journal, 63
National Labor Relations Act, 82
National League of Cities, 59
National Low Income Housing Coalition, 58
National Organization for Women, 100
National Research Council, 116
National Rural Housing Coalition, 58
National School Lunch Act, 52
National Youth Administration, 82
Neas, R., 98
Neighborhood Youth Corps, 27, 28, 89
New Careers, 89
New Deal, 76, 79-80, 82, 133
New Right, the, 4
New York Children's Aid Society, 118
New York Society for the Prevention of Cruelty to Children, 118
New York Times, 8, 15

Nixon, R., 43, 69, 89, 121, 141
Norris-LaGuardia Act, 82
Nutrition Education and Training Program, 52

Office of Economic Opportunity, 88-89
Office of Federal Contract Compliance, 95
Office of Technology Assessment, 115
Official poverty level, 21
O'Hara, J., 125
Okun, A., 138
Older American Act, 37
Operation Mainstream, 89

Panetta, L., 46
Parental leave, 102, 116, 123, 124, 130
Part-time workers, 83-84, 103
Pay equity, 93, 101-102
Peirce, N., 9, 72
Perkins, F., 3
Peterson, P., 6
Physicians Task Force on Hunger, 45, 47
Pierce, S. R., Jr., 66, 75
Pifer, A., 5, 9
Poage, W. R., 43
Polit, D., 125
Poor, the, viii, 11, 13, 26
Poor Peoples' Campaign, 43
Poverty, 5, 7, 21, 88, 111-112, 113, 114, 120, 123, 127, 128, 131, 133, 135, 141, 142-143
Poverty, Senate Subcommittee on, 43
Powell, L., Jr., 100
Pregnancy Discrimination Act, 96
President's Task Force on Food Assistance, 45-46
Private Industry Councils (PICs), 90
Privatization, viii, 5, 10, 66
Productivity, 14-15, 106, 143
Program for Better Jobs and Income, 121
Prudential Insurance, 72
Pruitt-Igoe, 65
Public employment, 77, 82-83, 121
Public housing, 3, 64-65, 68
Public Works Administration, 82
Public Works Employment Act of 1977, 96-97

Quotas, 96, 97, 98, 106

Reagan, R., viii, 4, 19, 39, 40, 43, 51, 60,
    66, 69-70, 71, 73, 74, 86, 91, 97, 98,
    105, 106, 117, 121, 141, 144
Reaganomics, viii
Reed v. Reed, 100
Reich, R., 140
Rent subsidies, 7, 66, 69, 70
Resolution Trust Corporation (RTC), 72
Retirement insurance, 33-34, 135
Reverse discrimination, 79, 96
Riemer, D., 103
Rios, P., 139
Rockefeller Foundation, the, 72
Rockwell International, 9
Roosevelt, E., 95
Roosevelt, F. D., 2-3, 30-31, 33, 80, 133
Roosevelt, T., 118
Rosen, D., 75
Rowan, C. T., 88
Ruggles, P., 141
Russ, M. A., 67

Savings and Loan bailout, 145
Schlesinger, A. M., Jr., 16, 17
School lunches, 3, 28, 37, 49, 51-52
Schorr, D., 126
Schorr, L., 126, 130
Segalonger, R., 7
Select committee on Nutrition and Human
    Needs, 43
Sex discrimination, 100-102
Shapiro, I., 127
Sheen, M., 57
Sheppard-Towner Act, 119
Silber, J. R., 118
Single-parent families, 14, 109, 111
Slaughter House Cases, the, 107n
Snyder, M., 57
Social assistance programs, 3, 31, 50, 78, 137
Social insurance programs, 3, 19, 31
Social Security, 4, 12, 13, 19, 83, 134
Social Security Act of 1935, 3, 30, 31-34,
    37, 119, 133
Solarz, S., 141

Sowell, T., 8, 13, 140
Star Wars, 145
Steele, S., 99
Stenholm, C., 124
Stewart, P., 97
Stone, M. E., 60
Sturdivant, J., 86
Summer Food Services Program, 52
Summer Youth Employment Program, 89
Supplemental Security Income (SSI), 13,
    35, 51, 136

Taft-Hartley Act, 82
Taxes, 10, 15, 24-25, 31-32, 60, 74, 134
Tax Reform Act of 1986, 24, 71, 75
Taylor, P., 132
Teenage pregnancy, 12
Thompson, T., 118, 134
Title VII, 95
Title IX, 96
"Trickle-down" theory, viii, 8, 66
TRW, 9

Unemployment, 81, 83-84, 142-143
Unemployment insurance, 12, 19, 35, 76,
    77, 83-84, 135
Unions, 82, 123
United States Advisory Board on Child Abuse
    and Neglect, 123
United States Bureau of Prisons, 89
United States Conference of Mayors, 43,
    57, 58
United States Steel, 9
United States v. Darby, 107n
United Steelworkers of America v. Weber,
    96
University of California Regents v. Bakke,
    96
Unwed mothers, 109-110, 117-118
Upward Bound, 28
Urban Coalition, 43
Urban Institute, 99
Urban renewal, 68

Veterans Administration, 67

Vietnam War, 3, 13, 29, 30
Volunteers in Service to America (VISTA), 27, 28
Voting Rights Act of 1965, 139

Walsh-Healey Act, 80
Wards Cove Packing Company v. Atonio, 98
War on Poverty, 3, 26, 27-30, 40, 50, 88, 133, 141
Watergate, 3, 13
Ways and Means, Committee on, 124
Weiner, L., 58, 59
Weisbrot, R., 98
Welfare class, 30, 117
Welfare dependency, 43, 48, 78, 117, 118, 120, 121
Welfare reform, 121
Welfare state, 1, 4, 18
West, D. A., 49
West Coast Hotel v. Parrish, 107n
White House Conference on Children, 118

White House Conference on Nutrition, 43
Wilder, D., 139
Wilson, P., 117
Wilson, W. J., 99
Women, Infants and Children Program (WIC), 37, 49, 52, 126, 128, 130
Women's Movement, 100
Women's rights, 13
Woodson, R. L., 99
Workers' compensation, 86
Workforce, 78, 89, 91-92, 125
Work Incentives Program (WIN), 122
Working mothers, 14, 115-116, 134
Works Progress Administration, 82
World War II, 3, 13, 14, 16, 67, 73, 82, 83, 86, 87, 140, 143
Wygant v. Jackson Board of Education, 98

"Yellow Dog" contracts, 82

Zigas, B., 58, 59

About the Author

Carl P. Chelf is Professor of Government at Western Kentucky University, where he has taught courses in American government and public policy for 30 years. He holds M.A. and Ph.D. degrees in political science from the University of Nebraska, Lincoln. He was a Congressional Fellow with the American Political Science Association in 1961-1962, working in the offices of Congressman John Brademas (D., IN) and Senator John Sherman Cooper (R., KY). In 1969-1970 Professor Chelf was an Academic Administrative Intern and Fellow with the American Council on Education. In 1971-1973 he was a Legislative Service Fellow of the American Political Science Association conducting orientation sessions and publishing a manual for freshman members of the Kentucky General Assembly. He has spent 18 years in various administrative positions at Western Kentucky University. His publications include *Political Parties in the United States,* with Thomas Madron (1974); *Public Policy-Making in America: Difficult Choices, Limited Solutions* (1982); *Congress in the American System* (1977); and *American Government: Kentucky Edition* (1991), with Barbara Conkle and Joel Goldstein. Professor Chelf is a member of the American

Political Science Association, the Policy Studies Organization, the Woodrow Wilson International Center for Scholars, and the Kentucky Political Science Association.